Look at like God

Maturing in Your Resemblance to Christ.

By Maranatha (Ogonna Nnaemeka)

Visitmaranatha.com

Biblical references and quotations include the use of the following versions: NLT (New Living Translation), KJV (King James' Version), CSB (Christian Standard Bible), MSG (The Message Translation), AMP (Amplified Version), NIV (New International Version), ESV (English Standard Version) and NIRV (New International Reader's Version).

Unattributed Charles Spurgeon quotes were taken from the KJV Spurgeon Study Bible.

Book Cover Creative Direction by Seun Badejo.

Book Cover Design by Rotimi Gbafe.

ISBN: 979-8-9871742-5-8
Published in 2025 by The Writer's Writer Studio
Thewriterswriter.org
hello@thewriterswriter.org

In partnership with
Onefirm Media Corp.
PO Box 186
New York, NY 10031

CONTENTS

DEDICATION

To my Abba, Yeshua and Helper, here we are again and only by Your Name. Thank You.

To Amanda, my perpetual cheerleader, you saw this book even when it had faded from my mind, and it came alive because of your encouragement. Thank you.

To my family, Daddy, Mummy, Emeka, Dhee, Sam and Joy —you have all held my pen to write with me in one way or the other. I love you all so much.

To Ebele, my dearest friend, you pored over this book, gently corrected my many errors—both theological and grammatical—and revived my hope when I felt this endeavour had turned pointless. Thank you.

To Kehinde, my best friend and partner for life, you never batted an eyelid when I asked you to read entire chapters over and again, nor did you relent to speak the truth for the greater good. Thank you for everything, but especially for lending me your eyes at a moment's notice.

To Maranatha, Sweet, Ogonna, Favour, and every other name you are called by. It has been quite a journey, and I am proud of how far He has brought you.

PRAYER

2 Corinthians 3:18 (KJV): But we all, with open face beholding as in a glass the glory of the Lord, are changed into the same image from glory to glory, even as by the Spirit of the Lord.

My prayer for you, as you read this book, is that you discover and embrace the paternity of God—no matter how terrible your experiences might have been with your earthly or parental figures, in Jesus' Name. Your heavenly Father loves and cares for you. He has made that choice to love you unconditionally, and He abides by His Word. May you accept this love.

—

'THIS IS A KIND OF KNOWLEDGE THAT COMES WITH FERVOUR. THE ZEAL OF THE LORD WILL DO IT.'

FOREWORD

There's a concept I've been turning over in my heart lately. It's something I've phrased, 'The Labour of the Righteous,' and it's my heart's attempt to contemplate which things actually bring delight to the Lord's heart. Our minds are wont to think of Dos and Don'ts when we ponder pleasing God, but if nothing else does, our utter exhaustion and periodic self-loathing from our repeated attempts and failures to 'do right by God' ought to tell us that we, at the very least, have the order wrong.

There's a detail we skip over too quickly in the famed Exodus 20, and I believe that pausing to pay rapt attention will make all the difference in the way the rest of the text is understood. The spotlight often rests on the Decalogue when we interact with Exodus 20, but I argue that the crown jewel of the text is the verse before the Ten Commandments are given: **'I am the LORD your God, who brought you out of Egypt, out of the land of slav-**

ery' (Exodus 20:2). Before the Lord calls the attention of His people to what He requires of them, He says to them, 'Look at Me; see who I am and contemplate what I have done.' And it's in the wake of the looking that God presents the doing, because the looking equips us for the doing, which then leads to the becoming. The righteous—the chosen, the set-apart, God's own people—will labour by looking first. The Bible says that it is impossible to please the Lord without faith, and faith's first vision is God. Noah, Abraham, Moses, David, Samuel ... all these men showed us that faith's first vision is God, and therefore, the true, pleasing labour of the righteous man begins with a looking.

As I read through Look At God Look Like God, I thought, *'Ah, someone understands the order as God intended it to be.'* This is a material for those who are weary of labouring in the flesh but know that there is a labour required regardless. The Lord will not change His mind; He wills for us to be conformed to the image of His Son **(Romans 8:29)**. It's the work He's perfecting in us every day. What Maranatha has done with this book is set the right order before us so that we can arrive at that intended end—the becoming. She has, with this work, pointed us to an involved God: a God who says, *'Behold Me, and become like Me.'* Not One who leaves us to struggle on our own, but One who draws near, who supplies grace, who takes our gaze off self-effort and fixes it on His Son.

This is the kind of book that steadies the heart, clarifies the path, and reminds us that we are not called to endless striving but to beholding. I'm convinced that you will find, as I did, that this work will steer you back to intimacy—the only place where true transformation happens.

My only counsel is to eat this book slowly; don't hurry through it. Come back to it as many times as you need to, because it is the kind of book you take your time to unravel.

May your vision of the Lord be unclouded, and may you be transformed to reflect His likeness more and more each day, until your life itself becomes a testimony of His glory.

Grace to you.

—Ebele Light-Akinosi,
Servant of God.

INTRODUCTION

Have you ever looked in the mirror expecting to see someone who is not you? My guess is no—unless you've stumbled into a badly written Hollywood horror movie. A mirror performs the primary function of reflecting an image of whatever object happens to face it.

In a way, this is the mirror we have come to study. But this mirror not only shows our reflection; it transforms it for our good and for the glory of God.

I first learned about this amazing mirror in **2 Corinthians 3:18 (KJV):**

> **But we all, with open face beholding as in a GLASS the glory of the Lord, are changed into the same image from glory to glory, even as by the Spirit of the Lord.**

When you receive salvation, the veil that blinded you to God is removed from your eyes (**2 Corinthians 4:4**). This is possible because the Spirit of the Lord, in whose presence freedom blissfully flourishes, makes it so. With this newfound emancipation in Christ, born of belief and repentance, we gain the ability to see the glory of God—the radiant sum of His divine attributes—something we could scarcely perceive beforehand.

What happens next? With an unveiled face, a contrite heart, and a thoroughly yielding and yearning spirit, we behold God as we spend time in fellowship with Him. But it does not end there—it's just the beginning.

The Amplified Version of **verse 18** above says, **'And we all, with unveiled face, continually seeing *as in* a MIRROR the glory of the Lord, are progressively being transformed into His image from [one degree of] glory to [even more] glory, which comes from the Lord, [who is] the Spirit.'**

Look at that! Just as we'd look into a mirror to find our reflection staring back at us, we can look in the same way to behold the glory of God—and be affected by it! The power of the Holy Spirit transforms God's children to look more and more like Him.

When we come before God, we seldom realise that we're gazing at the face of the One whose image we bear—our first Father who shared Himself with us to make us who we are. In truth, God is the mirror that reveals not just what we think we look like but who we really are, in Him, each person to themselves. As Scripture implies, our vision of His glory is only mirror-like—imperfect [incomplete] and limited, just as our [spiritual] sight is. Yet in His love, God steps in to help our sight, by faith, until the perfect comes.

Reader, beware: we are not looking into this mirror expecting to see our own reflection. We are not staring at God to find our anxious, self-absorbed selves, scarred by the burdens of this broken world, looking back at us. We do not behold God to have our opinions confirmed or our assumptions blessed.

No. We behold God for the revelation of our truest self —the one not defined by the world, but by His Word. We look at Him so we may look like Him—filled with and living out love, joy, peace, and every fruit of His Spirit, radiating holiness. We fix our gaze on our Father to learn who we truly are as His children.

Who are you, then? In this book—moving back and forth between the past, present, and future in three parts: *Creation*, *Distortion* and *Conformity*—my prayer is that you find yourself as a child again before your Father: yielded, nurtured, and maturing in resemblance to Him, even as you enjoy Him.

I have written this book for you as much as for myself. May it serve as one of many gentle reminders [albeit with fresh context to foster a renewed understanding] of God's steadfast love for you and your enduring hope in Him—for today and for every tomorrow, until you see Him face to face.

—Maranatha,
Your sister in Christ.

CREATION

1

A CHIP OFF THE OL' BLOCK

When a child is born, and his features are examined to reveal similarities between the child and the parent, happiness ensues. Otherwise, a bit of patient endurance must come to play—but it must happen. If it does not, there is trouble.
—Maranatha

Whenever I see a child, the first thing I subconsciously do is check who the child physically takes after. Does the child bear their mother's eyes or their father's smile? The answer may have no drastic or life-changing effect, but it quickly confirms where the child comes from—and to whom they belong.

This is how God made Adam (us)—in His likeness. The creation story narrates God's heart behind the creation of humanity.

Genesis 1:26 (KJV):
And God said, Let us make man in our image, after our likeness: and let them have dominion over the fish of the sea, and over the fowl of the air, and over the cattle, and over all the earth, and over every creeping thing that creepeth upon the earth.

How did God make humans? In His likeness. What did He make us for? To entrust us with dominion over the earth. God delegated authority, placing man (Adam) in charge of the earth.

When I say 'us', I am not referring to just Christians but *all* humanity. Every person you encounter carries the imprint of God's likeness.

These may sound like simple truths, yet they hold the power to free us from the narrow thinking that limits how we perceive God's fatherhood and our calling as His children on earth.

How? They answer two questions I have heard in many forms over the years—questions that have echoed since I was born: **'Who am I' and 'What am I here on earth for?'**

The creation story answers these questions perfectly, but it can seem shallow if one reads it as *just* a story—something familiar but not living. Within those first words of Genesis lies the truth about who we are and why we are here.

Who are you? You are a child of God, made in the image of God.

Why are you on earth? From the beginning, God made Adam to have dominion over the earth **(Genesis 1:28)** to fulfil His purpose and carry out His word. God made you to be like Him, to reflect His image.

I see God making us in His likeness as both a feature and a responsibility: a feature because it defines who we are, and a responsibility because it calls us to live as He is: holy, loving and steadfast.

Psalm 115:16 (AMP):
The heavens are the heavens of the Lord,
But the earth He has given to the children of men.

How beautiful is this knowledge? It may appear straightforward, even a tad bit bland, but *God is in the details*. The simplest things often hold the deepest realities —easily missed, not because they are hidden, but because they are so wonderfully plain.

You may have noticed that humans aren't the strongest creatures on earth (that would be the lion, perhaps) or the fastest (cheetahs easily outrun us). Yet, we occupy the top of the food chain. Why? Because God appointed us as stewards over the earth.

Did you know? God did not send rain because there was no one to tend the earth **(Genesis 2:5–6).** After He created man, He placed him in the garden to *work* the land and care for it **(Genesis 2:15; Genesis 1:26)**.

Even after the Fall, God, in His mercy, did not remove this dominion. Only now, our relationship with creation is tinged with fear, rather than the harmony and loving interaction that God intended **(Psalm 8:8–6; Genesis 9:2; 2:19–20)**.

'A chip off the ol' block' is a phrase used to describe a child who resembles their parent either in character or behaviour. This was God's idea when He created you. He made you in His likeness so that you might reflect Him.

Genesis 1:26 (AMP):
Then God said, "Let Us (Father, Son, Holy Spirit) make man in Our image, according to Our likeness [not physical, but a spiritual personality and moral likeness]."

Deity and humanity are not at odds. Our human bodies, this remarkable design, are gifts of God, entrusted to us for life on earth. All of creation flows from God and draws its existence from His power. But with humanity, God went a bit further—sharing intimate parts of Himself with us because of His deep love for us.

God—creating us in His image—went beyond giving us a physical form. God imparted three distinct qualities of His own being with us, marking humans as unique beings among earthlings: **personality, morality and spirituality**. We have distinct personalities that distinguish one person from another; we have a moral compass that guides our behaviour; and we have not just an outer part (our bodies) but an inner part (our souls/spirits). So, we may not physically resemble God [the Father], since He is Spirit, but we do in other ways.

God is invisible. In our frailty, the human mind often tries to assign a specific image to His divinity. This is why the second commandment warns, '**Thou shalt not make unto thee any graven image, or any likeness of any thing that is in heaven above, or that is in the earth beneath, or that is in the water under the earth' (Exodus 20:4).**

Idolatry occurs when God is falsely represented through a physical or mental image. Block,[1] commenting on the Prophet Ezekiel's vision of God's throne in Ezekiel 1, notes: '*Unlike the gods of the nations depicted on ancient seals and carvings, the glory of Yahweh defies human description, verbally or visually. And unlike the images of the heathen, which require constant attention and polishing, Yahweh's radiance emanates from His very being.*'

God's essence transcends every image we could create, yet He graciously reveals Himself in ways we can understand—one of which is through our own existence. In Ezekiel's vision of God's throne, many aspects of His form appeared human **(Ezekiel 1:5, 8, 26)**, Feinberg[2] observes: '*If God is to be portrayed in concrete form, the highest symbol man can use is the human form. When God wanted to reveal Himself in the supreme revelation of His person, He did so in the form of the Man Christ Jesus.*'

---

1. The Book of Ezekiel, Chapters 1–24 by Daniel I. Block.
2. The Prophecy of Ezekiel: The Glory of the Lord by Charles L. Feinberg.

But let us be clear about our resemblance to God—we are only a picture of Him. C.S. Lewis, in *Mere Christianity*, describes this resemblance most distinctly. Please, pay close attention:

> 'We don't use the words begetting or begotten much in modern English, but everyone still knows what they mean. To beget is to become the father of: to create is to make. And the difference is this.*
>
> *When you beget, you beget something of the same kind as yourself. A man begets human babies, a beaver begets little beavers and a bird begets eggs which turn into little birds. But when you make, you make something of a different kind from yourself. A bird makes a nest, a beaver builds a dam, a man makes a wireless set—or he may make something more like himself than a wireless set: say, a statue. If he is a clever enough carver he may make a statue which is very like a man indeed. But, of course, it is not a real man; it only looks like one. It cannot breathe or think. It is not alive.*
>
> *What God begets is God; just as what man begets is man. What God creates is not God; just as what man makes is not man. That is why men are not Sons of God in the sense that Christ is. They may be like God in certain ways, but they are not things of the same kind. They are more like statues or pictures of God.*
>
> *A statue has the shape of a man but is not alive. In the same way, man has the 'shape' or likeness of God, but he has not got the kind of life God has.*

> *Everything God has made has some likeness to Himself. The intense activity and fertility of the insects, for example, is a first dim resemblance to the unceasing activity and the creativeness of God. In the higher mammals we get the beginnings of instinctive affection.*
>
> *That is not the same thing as the love that exists in God: but it is like it—rather in the way that a picture drawn on a flat piece of paper can nevertheless be 'like' a landscape. When we come to man, the highest of the animals, we get the completest resemblance to God which we know of. Man not only lives, but loves and reasons: biological life reaches its highest known level in him.'*

Since we are made in God's image, it follows that His likeness is reflected in ours. I explain it this way so it is easier to grasp, even though it is backward, like saying a father resembles his child when it is actually the child who takes after the father. We draw from God's nature, partake of His being, and reflect Him—never the other way around.

His actions are holy replicas—again, in that backward way, for we are the imitators, not the source—of the things we would do ourselves. We often forget that we bear His image and that because we resemble Him, our actions echo His character. This is the core of who we are.

When we accuse God of withholding goodness until His best time, do we not see that we would do the same for those we love? Would we not discipline a child rather than have them go astray? Do we not delight in gifts that cost the conferrer dearly, just as God delights when we offer to Him sacrificially?

Our anger at injustice, fueled by our sense of justice, is an inheritance from our perfectly just Creator.

Our genuine acts of love are mere shadows of what God would do. In all of this, we see it clearly: WE TAKE AFTER HIM!

Matthew 7:11 (KJV):
If ye then, being evil, know how to give good gifts unto your children, how much more shall your Father which is in heaven give good things to them that ask him?

Time and again, the Bible holds up humanity as a mirror of God. We uphold His likeness in ways we do not realise. Our DNA is Him.

Even God's existence as a loving community—the Trinity—evinces something about our social nature. We are designed for connection, not isolation; loneliness is unnatural to the human soul. Adam's solitariness in the garden was the one thing that God declared to be *'not good,'* so He made Eve, the woman, as one fit for him.

Yes, we can seek out quiet times to meditate and declutter our souls from the noise of the world, but for the most part, our lives are intertwined with the lives of others and rightly so. We need one another, and we are needed in return.

As Timothy S. Lane and David Tripp, in *Relationships: a Mess Worth Making,* observe: *'Despite the fact that we are selfish people in a fallen world, our lives still reveal God's likeness. God is a community and we as His creation reflect this quality. Moreover, He brings us into community (right from when we are born, we belong in a family) and places the desire for community within us.'* In God, we find the perfect model of relational living.

As a child depends on a parent, God designed us to depend on Him. Adam experienced this reliance fully in a true, thriving fellowship with God. There was no hiding from God. Aside from sharing His nature with Adam, God also gave him meaningful work, made material provision for his well-being, and designed for him a helper, Eve, to complete him. God brought each animal He created to Adam to see what he would name it **(Genesis 2)**, and we also see an instance of God visiting the garden in the evening to walk and talk with Adam **(Genesis 3:8)**. This was pure intimacy, a friendship between God and man.

God intended that when we gaze upon Him, we see our true selves, and when He looks upon us, He beholds a part of Himself. Always sharing, always entwined; woven together in that tender, unbreakable bond of family.

The apple doesn't fall far from the tree. We are God's children—*chips off the ol' block*. We belong to God. We bear His likeness, embody His character, and live as reminders of His love. He is our Father, and, in Him, we find our truest identity.

2

THE SOURCE OF EVERYTHING GOOD

If the works of my hand produce confusion or anything less than what is 'good,' I would tear them down, again and again, until something good comes forth.

—Maranatha

God saw that all He had made was good.

Genesis 1:31 (NLT):
Then God looked over all he had made, and he saw that it was very good!

WHAT A COMFORT. What a joy.

It was the end of the sixth day, and God was pulling

down His sleeves and dusting His palms as He surveyed the fullness of His handiwork. He was pleased with what He saw. There the earth was ... sitting lushly below the heavens and brimming beautifully with animals, plants and the humans God had set over them. It was *all* GOOD.

What does 'good' mean, though? Does it connote how we'd describe a pleasant day: '*I had a good day today,*' or even a satisfying meal: '*The food was really good*'? The word 'good' here is the Hebrew word /ṭôḇ/ pronounced 'tov' (as in 'stove'), which means something *pleasant, agreeable, nice,* and *beautiful.* It is a compact word in which every positive word we often use can be found. But at its depth [as it relates to creation] it describes *'something that fulfils the purpose for which it was created'* —Terry Storch.[1]

This is the good that God saw—the perfection of design meeting intention.

God commanded humans (Adam and Eve) to govern the earth and rule over everything He'd made.

Genesis 1:28 (NLT):
28 Then God blessed them and said, "Be fruitful and multiply. Fill the earth and govern it. Reign over the fish in the sea, the birds in the sky, and all the animals that scurry along the ground."

In blessing the earth, He shared with us a measure of His own life-producing power according to His design. It is why God only needed to make the male and female of

1. Terry Storch, Tov Leadership (Newsletter, 29/07/2022).

each kind and entrust them with split seeds of a whole, which, when joined together, would create another life. He did not need to fashion every human being from dust like He did with Adam or Eve. Instead, to reflect a transfer of His creative and life-producing ability, He gave the first humans the capacity to reproduce. The same blessing rests upon animals and plants.

This is where our innovative capabilities come from, too. Beyond procreation, it is why human beings can conceive something in the mind and bring it to reality. Cars, light bulbs, and other technological advancements —these are manifestations of that creative imprint God placed within us.

It is a matter of fact, then, that we can find God in everything. His Word is the pulse that keeps the earth alive. He wove aspects of Himself into everything that He created, from the endless activity in animals to the persistence of heavenly bodies. He said, '*Let there be ...*' and there was; He hasn't withdrawn His Word ... at least not yet. It is Adonai's breath in our lungs. His active Word is what powers our speech, our strides, our movements ... everything that we do. We wake up each morning because He chooses to restore our souls within us again. The day He withholds life from us, we will be no more. You are reading these very lines because it pleased God to let it happen. If He were to take back His Word concerning creation, everything—every creature, every mountain, every human—would go back to dust in way less time than it would take to blink.

God's Word is not merely a spoken command, the way we understand words in human language. It is more like a *willing*. God *willed* the world into existence; His speech carried the full force of His intention. Nothing about this has changed today. His Word still contains the power of His will—what He purposes, He speaks, and what He speaks, He accomplishes.

His Word is His will. In the creation story, God talks to nothingness—a void and empty earth—and it understands His intentions even though it has never known life or light before. You need to understand this: the Word of God is the power that communicates with what does not yet exist, and it responds in fulfilment of what He has commanded. His Word is so powerful that it not only gives a command, it imparts the very ability to obey the command! It is like a deaf person who has never heard before, but when the Word says *'ears be opened,'* his ears instantly receive the capacity to hear even though they have never heard before! The power to obey is nestled within the instruction itself. God communicated His will to the earth, and it understood and obeyed.

In the book of Job, chapters 38 to 41, we witness God humbling Job, and through this divine reprimand, we gain a glorious glimpse of His awe-inspiring power over the earth. Here is a snippet:

Job 38:12–14 (NLT):
12 Have you ever commanded the morning to appear and caused the dawn to rise in the east?
13 Have you made daylight spread to the ends of the earth, to bring an end to the night's wickedness?

14 As the light approaches, the earth takes shape like clay pressed beneath a seal; it is robed in brilliant colors.

God commands the morning to awake and watches the earth stir at His will. From the heavens, He sees creation yawn into shape, shifting and stretching itself for another 24 hours—just as clay changes form beneath a seal. Many things we see in the universe are breathtaking, from the Aurora Borealis to Victoria Falls and even in space, but only God has seen the true glory of the earth. How awesome He is!

In **Exodus 3:14,** when God sends Moses to the Egyptians, He describes Himself as **'I AM'**. In **Hebrews 11:6**, we again see this same truth declared: **'He IS'**. Some translations render this as **'He exists'**, but the emphasis is on the fact that God exists outside context, category or comparison. He is not anything; He is everything! He does not exist as something—He is existence itself. And it is because He *is* that everything else can *be*—humans, animals, heavenly bodies, etc. His existence is what gives possibility, shape, and substance to ours.

As David pondered on the sheer weight of God's omniscience and omnipotence, he could only exhale in awe: '**Such [infinite] knowledge is too wonderful for me; It is too high [above me], I cannot reach it' (Psalm 139:6, AMP)**. And truly, it is too high for us—far beyond the reach of human comprehension. Everything we know of God is what He graciously unveils, and even that little—when we dare to meditate on it—can feel utterly overwhelming. It is high above us! Even as you read this book, you must take many descriptions and analogies as merely feeble attempts to gesture towards glorious realities too majestic for human language.

The world is beautiful because God is beautiful. Music is beautiful because God is beautiful. Every lovely thing you admire or enjoy is only a dim reverberation of God's holiness and glory, a whisper of His nature: the handsomeness of a young man, the innocence of a newborn baby, the delicate shape of a pregnant woman, the sweetness of Jollof rice, the satisfaction you get when an outfit in your head actually *slaps*[2] in real life, etc. All goodness streams from one source—our good, good God. He is our Father but also the Father of the entire universe, clothing the lilies and feeding the sparrows **(Matthew 6:26, 28)**. If you look at anything and soundly judge it as good, that is you looking at God, in a sense. If you enjoy anything in this world, what you're really enjoying is God. Again, if God were to withdraw Himself from this world, we would not only lose the ability to enjoy anything, but we would also dissipate into pre-Adamic nothingness.

I remember listening to a particularly ethereal song and a thought rose in my heart: if music on this fallen earth could lift the soul and make the spirit come alive, albeit temporarily, then what must the songs of Heaven accomplish? If melodies born in a broken world can sound so enchanting, then what auditory perfection awaits us in Heaven, where God, the source of it all, is enthroned? It must be magnificent. It must be glorious. It

2. Modern slang connoting approval or the exceptional goodness of something.

must defy every earthly word I could possibly think of! Perhaps I will find the words when I finally get to Heaven. *Tell you when I see you there, ok?*

There used to be no room in my mind for a joyful God —a *happy* God. I couldn't imagine a God who could smile, laugh or have a sense of humour. How mistaken I was! God is perfect happiness; perfect delight! Think about it: If you can laugh, crack jokes, be sarcastic and enjoy the bliss of good humour, does it not make sense that the excellence of those things exists in the God who is your source?

In truth, God is holy and in his holiness are gathered all His perfections—His joy, satisfaction, justice, etc. He is utterly pleased in Himself and His purpose. Our capacity to comprehend Him simply falls way below!

Charles Spurgeon captures it beautifully:

'Consider next the eternal purpose of God that he would create. He determines it in his mind. Could any but a divine motive actuate the divine architect? What must that motive have been? He creates that he may display his own perfections. He does beget, as it were, creatures after his own image that he may live in them—that he may manifest to others the joy, the pleasure, the satisfaction he so intensely feels in himself. I am certain his own glory must have been the end he had in view. He would reveal his glory to the sons of men, to angels, and to such creatures as he had formed in order that they might reflect his honor and sing his praise.'

This is the God we belong to—holy, happy, and

radiant in His own perfection, yet ever delighted to reveal and share His joy through the works of His hands.

God does not begin to be happy or joyful in the way our emotions often oscillate; He just *is*. It is the same way that He does not begin to exist, as we do; He simply exists. He is perpetual and eternal ... and everything about Him reflects that constancy. This is why Scripture declares that the Lamb was slain from the foundations of the world **(Revelation 13:8)**. For us, with our little minds, events unfold in time **(Galatians 4:4)**; for God, who is outside time, all things simply are.

It is because He is cheerful that we can be cheerful—often smiling, laughing or using pleasant words and gestures to express our delight. We resemble Him, remember? He is the perfection of happiness, joy, laughter ... **Zephaniah 3:17** says that God rejoices over us with singing! And it is not that God is happy or smiles in the same human way that we do, but that our happiness and smiles are only an expression of His holy and glorious delight.

He is the source of everything good. He is the *first* good. As St. Augustine prayed:

'O Lord, everything good in me is due to You.
The rest is my fault.[3]'

3. Augustine, Aurelius: Bishop of Hippo, the Confessions, book X. Paraphrased by Creed Confessions from the original text: *'The good I do is done by you in me and by your grace: the evil is my fault; it is the punishment you send me.'*

3

HEAVEN VS EARTH

Here is a place where my heart longs for when this fallen earth fills me with woe—Heaven.

—Maranatha

In the beginning, God created the heavens and the earth **(Genesis 1:1)**. [We know that He resides in Heaven now, but before the heavens came into being, where did He reside? Only God knows.]

When Scripture tells us that the earth was dark, void of form and not yet in use, it isn't describing an oversight —it's describing a canvas. Even though God created man last, He had Adam in mind from the instant He gave the first command for light to appear on the earth.

From the foregoing, it would seem that God creates the environment before the creature, ensuring that the creature is compatible with where it is supposed to dwell.

He formed the sky before He hung the stars, gathered the waters before creating the fish, and stretched out the earth before He shaped man. Each creature draws its essence from its primary environment, so it can thrive, multiply and fulfil purpose within it.

Adam was made from the dust of the earth before the Lord breathed life into him to make him a living being **(Genesis 2:7)**. Every creature we see today was lovingly formed by God Himself, from the stripes on a tiger to the gestation period of an elephant, from the intricate vision of an eagle to the blindness of a bat. All the wonders we studied in Biology class are simply glimpses into the intelligence, intentionality and artistry of God.

But as beautiful as the earth is, Scripture lets us know that it is only a copy of the things in Heaven.

Heaven, where God dwells, is a perfect harmony of elements. It is the one place where God's will is always done **(Matthew 6:10)**; a realm of aesthetic excellence, wholly holy, where the tangible presence of God is held in unbroken awe, day in and day out **(Revelation 4)**.

As God created us in His likeness, the earth also carries reflections of Heaven, where He resides. When Scripture says there is rejoicing in Heaven over a repentant sinner **(Luke 15:7)**, it resonates with what we understand on earth because God shared that quality of joy between both realms. Heaven and earth rejoice because the God, who fills both, rejoices.

We see in the Bible dazzling hints of heavenly elements that mirror what we know on earth, from gates, thunder, and songs, to gold and other precious stones. Since the heavens preceded the earth, and both sprang from the same eternal source, it is little wonder that they carry similar features. Yet, what we see on earth is but a dim reflection of God's glory in Heaven.

Adam Clarke[1] simplifies this further in his commentary on **Matthew 6**: *'But why is it called the kingdom of Heaven? Because God designed that his kingdom of grace here should resemble the kingdom of glory above. And hence our Lord teaches us to pray, Thy will be done on earth, as it is in Heaven.'*

Still, we must remember that while earth still bears traces of Heaven, Heaven remains uncorrupted; it is untouched by sin, decay or brokenness. So even where earth mirrors certain heavenly realities, Heaven holds the purer and truer version. If Earth is an echo, Heaven is the melody. It is important to hold this close to heart so that when some earthly beauty enraptures us, and we are tempted to lay up frail, material treasures, anchoring our affections on the things that glitter but do not last, we remind ourselves that such things are only signposts, not the destination. It is in Heaven we must lay up our treasures **(Matthew 6:19–21)**, for Heaven is our true inheritance. '*Heaven is the goal.*'

Let us take our understanding even further: in **Matthew 18:18–20**, we see that the word 'heavenly' can sometimes refer to the *spiritual* realm. Scripture uses it in both a positive and a negative sense. Paul, for instance, says that believers are blessed with every spiritual blessing and seated with Christ in the heavenly places

---

1. The Adam Clarke Commentary: Commentary on Matthew 6 by Adam Clarke.

(Ephesians 1:3; 2:6), referring to the spiritual position of the believer. In **Ephesians 6:12**, it describes spiritual wickedness in heavenly places. Although another discourse on its own, we know that, in this way, the spiritual realm animates the physical realm and what we see with our eyes is shaped by realities we cannot see.

This deduction checks out for several reasons: First, we are spirit/soul housed in a physical body, often referred to as the flesh **(1 Thessalonians 5:23; Matthew 10:28; 1 Corinthians 7:34; 5:5)**. Since God is a Spirit **(John 4:24)**, and we are made in His image, it follows naturally that we carry an inner being (spirit/soul) that animates our physical bodies, which were designed to inhabit the earth.

Second, the Psalmist hinted at this mystery when he wrote about God creating his innermost being in **Psalm 139:13**. He is clearly not referring to bone or skin, but that invisible part of us that feels eternity's tug.

In addition, we can trace our creative functionality to this truth: the invisible precedes what is visible, for do we not ideate before we create? This signifies intelligence, a trait of the divine shared with humanity. Animals and plants do not possess this. They are moved by instincts, not inspiration—a chameleon does not dream up new colours, it simply reacts to danger.

When God called the Israelites out of Egypt to worship Him, He did not leave Moses to guess what that worship should look like. He, instead, unfolded a heavenly blueprint for Moses to replicate, from the Mercy Seat to the cherubim. What Moses built was only an imitation of something far more perfect, existing in Heaven. The earthly tabernacle was patterned after a heavenly reality that would pull their gazes upward to look at He who was truly perfect and glorious.

God instructed Moses, '**Be sure that you make everything according to the pattern I have shown you here on the mountain' (Exodus 25:40, NLT).** The New Testament cast a brighter light on this command, where it says, '**These serve as a copy and shadow of the heavenly things, as Moses was warned when he was about to complete the tabernacle. For God said, 'Be careful that you make everything according to the pattern that was shown to you on the mountain' (Hebrews 8:5, CSB).**

Even in our modern day, we keep reaching upward, trying to create a semblance of Heaven in our worship—majestic and imposing church architecture, solemn and sober chords, etc. And when we experience something that seems too pure for this fallen earth, what do we say? *'It feels like Heaven.'* How do we know? Have we been there before? Exactly.

What we call 'creation' or 'manifestation' is then, in truth, more like a transportation—a movement of what God has ordained in eternity into the realm of time where our physical eyes can behold it.

When God said, '**Let there be ...**' His Word was already a completed reality in His will. What remained was for that finished reality to appear in time and take on physical form on the earth.

It is why Scripture can say that Jesus Christ was slain from the foundations of the world **(Revelation 13:8)**; yet His crucifixion still unfolded within history, at an appointed moment, in the fullness of time **(Galatians 4:4)**.

The eternal will of God stepped into the timeline of humanity.

When God told Abraham that he would have descendants beyond number, that promise was sealed the moment God spoke it. Yet, it was at God's appointed time that it happened.

We also see an example of this in Daniel's experience in **Daniel 10.** From the moment Daniel prayed, God heard him and sent an answer through an angel (transportation). However, Daniel's receipt of the answer was delayed because wicked spiritual forces resisted the messenger. *(I include this example carefully because, unlike Daniel's time, the believer today stands under a greater covenant. We have a victorious Advocate in Heaven—one whose death and resurrection dismantled the authority of the devil and stripped his power—so the believer need not fear such a situation like in Daniel's case. We will explore this in later chapters.)*

Job's story provides another instance—his trials were *approved* in the unseen before any sorrows reached him **(Job 1)**.

However, let this be clear to you: this does not mean that one realm is *weaker* or *lesser* than the other. Both were crafted by the same God, and both carry out His purposes, even in a world now tainted by the fall of man. By God's grace, the story gets even better! For in due time, everything will be renewed: we will receive new bodies **(1 Corinthians 15)**, and there will be a new earth **(Revelation 21)**, even as our inner man (spirit/soul) reaches the perfection of sanctification—but more on this later.

At the very least, then, we can take comfort, even joy, in knowing that what is possible for us is not limited to our material conception. Our vision is painfully small, narrowed by our spiritual myopia; we make many mistakes in both our desires and petitions. Fortunately, God is able to do far more than we could ever ask or think **(Ephesians 3:20)**. Where we want the wrong things, He withholds them and gives us what is good. Where we fumble in prayer, He intercedes for us with a compassion that understands our frailty more than we ever could **(Hebrews 7:25)**.

This much is obvious, then, that eternity speaks and time catches up. For us now, this transportation happens [through prayer, obedience, the hands of other humans; or sometimes through a combination of all] when we come into true and uncompromising alignment with the will of God, by faith, just like Abraham and all the other heroes of faith **(Hebrews 11)**. And while faith is principal in coming before God, we must guard our minds from thinking that it is our faith in itself that makes things happen. Our faith does not make God's will happen. For it is less about the strength of our faith and more about the object of our faith. That I don't believe in Paracetamol pills won't stop them from curing my headache if I take them as prescribed.

If we are honest, we know intimately the countless times we have doubted, hesitated, disbelieved, and yet God, in His mercy, still brought His Word to pass. Faith is only an ordained means, a gift through which God chooses to work. It is by His will that our faith means anything at all. Having faith in God's will is obedience that breeds commendation from Him.

So, back to the matter; believe it or not, this fallen

earth that we complain about almost every waking minute was once a perfectly beautiful and stable place. It mirrored Heaven in purity. And you, too, created to reflect your loving, holy Father, God in Heaven, were once completely in sync with Him.

In the beginning, man lived in intimate connection with God. He had no sin, and so he could commune with God face to face. The Lord brought creatures to Adam to name them **(Genesis 2:19)**! There was a pure bond between the soul/spirit and body. There was no inner division, or guessing, or wrestling; no *'is this me or is this God?'* There was no faith versus sight. Faith was sight and sight was faith.

There was perfect synchrony. Heaven and earth were not at odds, and neither were we; the body wasn't resisting the spirit, nor the spirit constantly trying to drag the body along. Everything moved in rhythm with God.

But then, something went terribly wrong ...

DISTORTION

4

SOMETHING'S OFF

That a child is disowned does not mean he stops looking like his father, at least physically.
—Maranatha

The end of the beginning unfolded in **Genesis 3**, when Adam and Eve devoured the fruit that contained death in its mesocarp. That tree was more than a forbidden *delicacy*; it was a choice—a decision to rule over themselves and *do* life apart from God, guided by their faulty wisdom. It was death, for a life without God is death. The results of eating the fruit would produce both spiritual and, eventually, natural death.

The world we live in now is a painful place to be in—a sharp contrast to the peace and joy in Eden. Every day, we face the loss of both people and things precious to us, and we wonder why. Good and evil wrestle, and good seems to lose more often than it wins. We witness injustice after injustice, and we wonder if there is a God in Heaven allowing all these things to happen.

However, the evil in this world has an origin: a choice made a long, long time ago by someone given the freedom to choose. This is why the battle between good and evil rages not just all around us, but most importantly, within us. In fact, we can trace the source of many evils around us to the evil within us.

As God settled man into Eden after creation, placing him there to tend to it and exercise the dominion He had entrusted to him, He issued Adam a clear warning: he was not to eat from a particular tree in the garden. This tree represented not just the knowledge of good and evil but also the profound providence of choice and free will by God.

Genesis 2:15–17 (AMP):
15 So the Lord God took the man [He had made] and settled him in the Garden of Eden to cultivate and keep it.
16 And the Lord God commanded the man, saying, "You may freely (unconditionally) eat [the fruit] from every tree of the garden;
17 but [only] from the tree of the knowledge (recognition) of good and evil you SHALL NOT eat, otherwise on the day that you eat from it, you shall most certainly die [because of your disobedience]."

Adam does disobey. Consequently, he dies spiritually

[losing eternal life] and God pronounces judgement on him and all who would come from him. God curses the serpent and the ground, puts enmity between the serpent's and woman's offspring, increases the woman's pain in childbirth, amongst other repercussions **(Genesis 3:14–19).**

For sin, God's beautiful creation becomes distorted in an instant; shame, guilt, blame-shifting, and enmity take root. Deep within you and me lies a strong propensity for evil because of sin.

Genesis 3:21 (NLT) says, **'The Lord God made clothing from animal skins for Adam and his wife.'** From the very beginning, (an) innocent animal(s) had to be sacrificed to cover the sins of the first humans. Here, we glimpse the foreshadowing of the Old Testament's system of atonement—a harbinger of an even more glorious plan to redeem the entire world **(Hebrews 10:1).**

Courtesy of sin, a new and faulty kind of awareness comes upon Adam and Eve, rendering them unfit for the perfection that is Eden. They had to leave. **Genesis 3:7 (AMP)** says, **'Then the eyes of the two of them were opened [that is, THEIR AWARENESS INCREASED], and they knew that they were naked; and they fastened fig leaves together and made themselves coverings.'**

What happened at the Fall went far beyond merely gaining the knowledge of good and evil; at its core was disobedience to God's command. Even a Godly instruction becomes disobedience if it is not performed at God's appointed time; how much more an outright refusal to obey?

If God had told them to stay away from the tree, there

must have been a purpose in it. We know that every command from God is for our own good **(Deuteronomy 10:13)**. Perhaps God would have given them its fruit to eat in due time; perhaps they just weren't mature enough to handle the burden of the knowledge of good and evil, so He warned them to keep their distance. Or perhaps they were never meant to eat the fruit of the Tree of the Knowledge of Good and Evil ... so many maybes. But the undeniable truth is that they chose their own way and stepped off the path that God had carved out for them.

We see the first signs of distortion in **Genesis 3:8–10 (NIRV)**; it is the children hiding from their Father:

> **8 Then the man and his wife heard the Lord God walking in the garden. It was during the coolest time of the day. They hid from the Lord God among the trees of the garden.**
> **9 But the Lord God called out to the man. "Where are you?" he asked.**
> **10 "I heard you in the garden," the man answered. "I was afraid, because I was naked. So I hid."**

Guilt produces a shame that stains the bond of intimacy. It drove the children to hide from the Father with whom they had once spoken freely; the Father they had delighted in, the Father they had looked upon with love. Instead, He appeared to them not as their source of joy but as their judgement and fright. They no longer recognised themselves when they looked at Him. Rather, they recoiled at the sight of holiness, for they no longer resembled God because of their sinful choice. They had become ... different from the Father.

This becomes the blight of all humanity—the condition we inherit simply by being born of Adam. Remember, God gave every one of His creations the ability to produce after their kind **(Genesis 1:24–25, 28)**. So, Adam's sin corrupted all who would ever come from him, for he was the first man. This is why every human being needs to be saved. We are not sinners because we sin; we sin because we are human (from Adam). Adam's sin became our inheritance, and everyone born of him stands condemned to die because of it, unless ...

The Father's heart broke, and as He beheld Adam and Eve closely for the last time in Eden, making clothes for them from the first innocent animals to die [for their high treason was only punishable by death and a substitute had to take their place] and setting a precedent for the sacrificial atonement for sins, He already knew how He would redeem the entire situation. Yet, He still had to send them out of the garden, lest they eat of the Tree of Life and remain spiritually dead forever **(Genesis 3:21–22)**. Imagine having the nature of sin and living forever? That would have been a true disaster. Bless the Lord that we can die, through Christ's death, and start over, through His resurrection!

We must note here that God, the Mirror, does not change. He never does **(Hebrews 13:8; Colossians 1:15)**. So, what changed? It is our sight that becomes impaired because of sin. We no longer behold God in the full range of (spiritual) vision as we should. Sin causes spiritual death and with it, a restriction of the intimate communication between man and God. Inevitably, our spiritual sight becomes hindered. This is the root of unbelief and fear.

Sin prevents a person from seeing and knowing God. It breeds doubt about our true origin. It closes the mind of the natural man to the existence of God. It makes us question His paternity and fatherhood towards us. Sin causes our actions to stand in direct contrast to God's, not solely intentionally but because we now rely on the ~~wisdom~~ foolishness that exists within the narrow bounds of our own faulty, so-called logical knowledge.

How can we even attempt to look at God when things have become this bad? To us, we look nothing like Him! He's *too* holy, *too* kind, *too* good to bear any resemblance to us. We're sullied, doing the very things we hate; doing wrong when we know what is right **(Romans 7:19, 21)**, stumbling into all sorts of blunders.

Within us, there is a war—a gaping hole. We feel no peace nor satisfaction, no matter how many *good* works we perform: charitable acts, pious displays, generous tithes and offerings. Our righteousness is but filthy rags **(Isaiah 64:6)**, because we are stained by sin, and even our purest motives are so often selfishness in disguise.

Adam and Eve knew they had sinned against God, and I cannot imagine the grief that swallowed them as they realised all they had lost. Yet, the distortion gets even worse. In the very next generation, with Cain and Abel, the first murder was committed **(Genesis 4)**. If this was the fruit at that time, how much more now?

What is the extent of this distortion?

5

SPIRITUAL BLINDNESS

It is better for a man to be blind and acknowledge his lack of sight than to be without sight and pretend he can see. One may receive the help he needs, the other has condemned himself to a life of folly.

—Maranatha

Many of us profess that God is omnipresent, omnipotent, and omniscient, yet our actions betray our belief. If you truly lived your life based on what you knew was true, would you play that carnal song spewing all manners of profanity because it is just *vibes*? I'd bet $10,000 that if you could see Jesus standing right beside you, you know He would not be *vibing* to that worldly music. But we take His omni-qualities for granted because we cannot see Him.

This is spiritual blindness, a consequence of the Fall

and our inability to perceive, let alone behold, God, even though He is everywhere. The Bible tells us that the earth is full of His glory **(Isaiah 6:3)**. Everything He has made reflects Him, for creation proclaims His handiwork **(Psalm 19)**.

What should be our actual stance?

2 Corinthians 4:18 (KJV) spells it out concisely:

> **While we look not at the things which are seen, but at the things which are not seen: for the things which are seen are temporal; but the things which are not seen are eternal.**

Our gaze should extend beyond the physical. Ideally, we were created to commune intimately with God. But we do not. Perceiving God can be quite the struggle. We wonder, *'Was that just my mind?'* or *'Was that God speaking?'* At the very beginning, there was no such uncertainty. It was simply God and man, in perfect communication and complete synchrony.

But sin changed things.

Distortion is a terrible effect of sin [the Fall]. We are still made in God's image, and so we long to be in His presence and hear His voice. Deep within us, there is a God-shaped void that only He can fill. Yet at the same time, we are so afraid of Him. He is infinitely holy, and we are profoundly sinful. We are not always conscious of this, but it is what emerges when we examine ourselves at the core. Just as we rarely appreciate the company of those with whom we're not alike in some way, so too do we struggle to approach the One who is entirely unlike us.

The distortion of God's image in man began with the distortion of God's Word. Consider what the serpent said to Eve about the forbidden fruit; he claimed she would '... **be like God, knowing [the difference between] good and evil' (Genesis 3:5, AMP).** Was he wrong? Not really. Was he right? Not really. As a master of deception, the serpent relied on half-truths, twisting God's Word and revising it to suit his cunning. From the very beginning, we see that it is imperative that we understand the Word of God for ourselves. Like the Bereans in **Acts 17**, we must examine the Word carefully to understand it, so we do not misapply it. We cannot simply accept something as Scripture because someone says it is. We must go see for ourselves, sitting under the guidance of the Spirit of God, to comprehend. It is so important!

We know the truth of the serpent's tales, don't we?

Rather than becoming 'like God' as Satan boldly promised, they actually became less like Him. The only way they resembled God was in knowing the difference between good and evil—a fat load of good that is doing us now!

Their eyes were indeed opened. The devil's trickery usually contains some element of truth; otherwise, it would not be deception. Consider, for example, the three temptations of Jesus **(Matthew 4)**; the devil was neither entirely wrong nor entirely right. The lesson is clear: we must flee anything that is not the whole Word and will of God. As Adam and Eve's eyes became open, the knowledge of good and evil came with the revelation of their own rebellion and sin, birthing guilt and shame. As their physical eyes opened, their spiritual sight dimmed.

We must pause here to unwrap Eve's disobedience. It followed a progression that reveals a common path of sin in our own lives—a path that veils God from us: distortion, doubt and dabbling.

Recall that this was God's specific instruction to Adam concerning the tree of the knowledge of good and evil.

Genesis 2:15–17 (CSB):

16 And the Lord God commanded the man, "You are free to eat from any tree of the garden,

17 but you must not eat from the tree of the knowledge of good and evil, for on the day you eat from it, you will certainly die."

In turn, here is Eve's version of the command:

Genesis 3:2–3 (CSB):

2 The woman said to the serpent, "We may eat the fruit from the trees in the garden.

3 But about the fruit of the tree in the middle of the garden, God said, "You must not eat it or TOUCH it, or you will die."

Now, we do not know how the idea of touching the fruit arose, for it is absent from God's original command to Adam. Perhaps Adam miscommunicated God's words to Eve. Perhaps Eve misunderstood what Adam said. We cannot be certain. But this is where the distortion began: God did not say that merely touching the fruit would bring death, yet that is what Eve recounts.

The devil started with a question, '**Did God really say,**

'You can't eat from any tree in the garden?' (Genesis 3:1, CSB). But of course, he knew full well that God never said that! God did not forbid them from eating of every tree in the garden, only a single, specific tree. Yet, the devil wages wars from the same starting point: against the Word of God and our understanding of it to plant doubt **(Matthew 13:19).**

Please, my friend, study God's Word and show yourself approved. Do not rely only on what you have been told because distortion does not always happen intentionally.

With God's Word being distorted to Eve, Satan proceeded to make her doubt it and, in doing so, doubt both the goodness of God and the evil of sin. *Why would He not want you to have something this good?* And remember, Eve believed that touching the fruit would bring death. Imagine her grabbing the fruit and nothing happening; this would only have strengthened her doubt in God!

Eve was enticed, she dabbled in sin, and she reaped the consequences. We often think that we can have a taste of sin and quickly rinse our mouths, but sin leaves a flavour that lingers, no matter how scant the portion we help ourselves to. Only the blood of Jesus can cleanse its tang **(Hebrews 10:22).**

My middle name is Sweet, and my family believes that I live up to the name due to my love for sweet things, especially confectionery. When I was younger, my mother tried to remedy the situation by giving me Yoyo Bitters, a polyherbal liquid tonic, said to aid detoxification. A strong-headed child, I outrightly refused. So, she negotiated: she bought me a pack of *5Alive* fruit juice and said I could have it all for just a small spoon of the bitter thing. I agreed, for such offers were scarce in my reality.

It was a nightmare. The taste of the bitters at the back of my tongue would not budge, even after several gulps of the *5Alive* juice. I cried bitterly, eyeing the Judas that my mother turned out to be. She knew the *5Alive* would do nothing to erase the bitterness. I brushed my tongue furiously, to no avail.

You know what saved me? Vitamin C tablets. I popped a couple, and though my tongue hurt from the battle between sharp and bitter, the unpleasant taste disappeared quickly.

When I think about it, Jesus is like that Vitamin C tablet and our works are like that *5Alive* juice.

2 Corinthians 4:4 (NKJV):
whose minds the god of this age has blinded,
who do not believe, lest the light of the
gospel of the glory of Christ, who is the
image of God, should shine on them.

Through sin comes the spiritual blindness that we now experience; this tainting of our souls and our loss of eternal life. We sin and think, *'it's not that deep,'* but the taste remains while its consequences ripple through time and affect the lives of others. People say, *'I don't need Jesus,'* and believe me, they *really* believe they don't. I know because I have been there. This is the blindness.

And Satan knows, he knows that we cannot truly appreciate God's sacrifice of His Son if we do not understand the brutal gravity of sin. Which is why the only evangelism that makes sense is one that zooms in on humanity's sin, and our desperate need for a Saviour.

This chapter has explored the source of sin on the earth and the dynamics at play so that you might understand, beyond the surface, how terrible and disastrous sin truly is.

Next, let us turn to some very relatable examples of spiritual blindness in our everyday lives—moments that lead us to forget, all too often, God's fatherly care for us and His purpose for our lives.

6

RESTRAINED

A prison is not merely an enclosed room with four walls, stern guards and no windows. It is also a beautiful castle that you cannot leave.

—Maranatha

Have you ever wondered how boring Heaven must be? All they do is sing to God and worship Him. What a bore! Don't they get tired? Don't they do other things? *And where, I ask, is the Jollof rice?*

Like many other Christians, I once had this perception of Heaven. I thought it must be boring, since all they did was sing. Hell, on the other hand, seemed more interesting—a continuation, I imagined, of the things we already do on earth.

How wrong—and silly—I was. While it is true that in

Heaven, there is perpetual worship of God **(Revelation 4:8)**, our perspective is flawed. Simply put, we're trying to understand spiritual realities from a fleshy, human point of view. If earth, fallen as it is, can hold such a delicate balance of joys and sorrows because of a perfect God who does not withhold His goodness despite our human wickedness **(Matthew 5:45)**, how much more must Heaven, where the source of everything good resides, surpass our understanding?

Another effect of sin is that it restrains our emotions and makes us incapable of experiencing the full and pure range of our feelings as God intended. How did God design things to be? A look at the fruit of the Spirit in **Galatians 5:22–23**: love, joy, peace, longsuffering, gentleness, goodness, faith, meekness and temperance, provides the answer. For God Himself is the perfection of emotions; He is perfect anger, perfect justice, perfect love, perfect happiness.

In contrast, and as a result of the Fall, we become angry and sin; we love and sin; we become afraid and sin. We express these emotions, yet at the end of each, we yield to sin rather than manifest pure feelings that glorify God **(Ephesians 4:26)**. These emotions are not inherently bad; it is our sinful nature that perverts them. The *cutest* part? We attach all sorts of labels to the various aspects of our fallen nature: *'I'm Choleric, I can't help being rude and bossy...'*

This restraint is why a person can confess *undying* love for another person, yet constantly violate or abuse them. We call this toxic love, but in truth, it is not love at all, just hate masquerading. It is also why we sometimes feel God is distant, even when Scripture reminds us that in Him we live and move and have our being, so He is certainly not far from us (**Acts 17:27–28**). It is why we imagine Heaven to be boring from our human perspective, judging it by the capabilities of our fallen flesh. When you really think about it, it is laughable to expect Heaven to be dull. This is the habitation of the same God who created the earth and, even after sin ruined it, we still find it beautiful and its creations valuable. How much more, then, must Heaven be, where He resides!

Psalm 16:11 assures us that at the Lord's right hand are pleasures forevermore. Have you ever wanted something so intensely that you thought you might die if you didn't get it, only to finally receive it and you're like, *'Is that it?'* I used to have this habit of constantly ordering stuff online, not because I particularly needed them, but because I loved the thrill of expecting a package. But the moment the parcel arrived, the desire evaporated, and I'd head back to Instagram looking for the next thing to buy.

Such is the perpetual cycle of earthly living under the shadow of sin. Everything here is laced with corruptible pleasures; the satisfaction from whatever we find here does not last. This is why we often find ourselves chasing one high after another; craving the next thing, the next thrill. But in Heaven, boredom is impossible. Our inheritance is '**... imperishable, undefiled, and unfading, kept in heaven for you' (1 Peter 1:4, CSB)**. Believe this, it is the surest promise you will ever receive!

Sin turns us into users. God designed us to steward the earth according to His will, loving Him and loving our neighbours, but we crave domination over other human beings. Think of how often you hear of people maltreating other people. Think of the slave trade, and how something so grotesque, so fundamentally evil, could have happened and persisted.

Sin makes us evaluate people not as image-bearers of God, but as commodities. We think of others in terms of the value they bring into our lives; how their presence might polish our own image, and how good we would look if they were with us. It is why we gravitate towards the beautiful or the wealthy, because their beauty and wealth add to ours by association. It is why we maintain ties with that wicked uncle, because he gives money, and we can say our uncle is *'so so and so'* whenever we need to brag and establish our relevance in the world's hierarchy. We want to *add* value to those who are valuable because it feels like a safer investment. That way, we have assurance of ROI since they have a track record. Sin teaches us to see human beings as leverage, as stepping stones, as assets ... because *'your network is your net worth.'*

(What a net worth Jesus must have had!)

We do not know how to be good, like God, who is good just for the sake of being, who loves wretched sinners like us that could offer Him nothing in return. Our finest efforts are, as St. Augustine puts it, *'splendid vices.'* Measured against one another, we might even look impressive, seemingly perfect, but comparison with people is a broken scale. It is only against God's holy standard that we see the truth: we all fall short.

We do not know how to delight in goodness for its own sake. We even use ourselves! We use our bodies, the beauty, intelligence and other gifts God has given to us, to perpetrate evil. Even our relationship with God often becomes one of constant grasping, where we attempt to use Him or force His hand for blessings. We do not worship God because He is worthy to be worshipped; we come before Him in exchange for blessings, upholding a transactional Christianity—blatant legalism. We linger in God's presence not to enjoy Him, but so we can say we prayed long. We stay to extract answers, spiritual strategies and blueprints, as though God does not know what we need anymore and must be directed. We want to *'pay the price,'* the cost of entry; our worship is our capital, and God is an investment from which we expect a return.

We attach ourselves to groups and communities that make us feel good, giving alms only to virtue-signal. We attend churches where the Word of God is freely added to and subtracted from, where His holiness is diminished, yet we do not leave because we love the prestige of belonging to a popular church and its *anointed* man of God. We stay because we believe our testimony is '*on the way*.'

We organise crusades not for salvation but for signs and wonders that point not to Christ but to the man of God. The man of God needs the hall full, and we need our miracles delivered quickly. God becomes a means to an end, the church another idol. The man of God does not truly care for us, and we do not truly care for him. It is why when a scandal breaks in church, our first impulse is not to pray but to gossip; and even when we pray, it is often only to protect our own interests. We never truly cared. It is why we find it easy to leave our Christianity at the door when our boss asks us to inflate figures at work or an opportunity appears to satisfy our lustful desires. We never really loved God or His commands.

We practice a Christianity that does not reach our hearts; our hearts stay stony. We lift *holy hands* in church on Sunday and practise wickedness every other day.

We are such terrible people because of sin, such deeply selfish people. But the tragedy is not merely that we are this way; it is that we do not even realise it! Our notorious, inflated self-image blinds us to the far-reaching consequences of our sin, and so we underestimate it. C.S. Lewis, in *Mere Christianity*, explains God's relationship with time, and his insight helps us understand, if only a little more, just how dreadful sin is:

> *'Almost certainly God is not in Time. His life does not consist of moments following one another. If a million people are praying to Him at ten-thirty tonight, He need not listen to them all in that one little snippet which we call ten-thirty.*
>
> *If you picture Time as a straight line along which we have to travel, then you must picture God as the whole page on which the line is drawn. We come to the parts of the line one by one: we have to leave A behind before we get to B, and cannot reach C until we leave B behind. God, from above or outside or all round, contains the whole line, and sees it all.'*

This concept of time is crucial in understanding why we so easily downplay our sins [and we should not]. We think in terms of past, present and future, but because God, the One whom we sin against, does not exist in time, He sees all our sins for all time at one time. Our past, present and future sins are already known by God. Since sin is not just the action but the potency, we must realise that when we see a seed, God sees the forest. With Adam, for example, God saw within his single act of disobedience the sins of the entire human race from the beginning until the Second Coming—his rebellion affected all. In the same vein, Christ's eventual sacrifice also atoned for the sins of all and for all time **(Romans 5:14–15)**.

Ponder this, too, and you will find it to be true. I can not remember everyone that I have hurt, but I can remember a fair number of the ways that people have hurt me. The one who is wounded likely remembers the transgression far better than the one who inflicted the wound. We might forget our sins because of the passage of time, but again, God's concept of time is not like ours.

And while we can barely see the full effects of our wrongdoing, God, being Almighty, knows exactly how catastrophic that *little lie* I told truly was. He sees every person touched by my actions and knows precisely how the hurt travelled their lives. He also knows how deeply my own sins corrode my own soul. He sees the ripple effect of every sin that we commit as it echoes through time.

How much better the world would be if the Church focused on helping people grasp the depth of their sins in light of the depth of God's love and holiness in salvation!

In the beginning, Adam had *Zoe*, a spiritual life of the same kind as the life of God—eternal life. After the Fall, however, every human born of Adam inherits only the natural life (*Bios*). This is much like a shadow of the *Zoe* life in the same way a sketched landscape is a shadow of an actual picturesque scenery—they have the same form, but one is only a picture (not really the real thing). Our natural lives are subject to corruption, death and decay; **'from dust to dust' (Genesis 3:19)** because of sin. By this nature, we are **'children of wrath' (Ephesians 2:3)**, separated from God and deserving of His judgement. In reconciling with God, this natural state must undergo a radical transformation through salvation in Christ alone. Salvation ushers us back into *Zoe* (Christ's life), making us co-heirs with Him. But that is only the beginning of the journey.

> **Colossians 3:9–10 (CSB):**
> **9 Do not lie to one another, since you have put off the old self with its practices**
> **10 and have put on the new self. You are being renewed in knowledge according to the image of your Creator.**

Even after we have put off the *old man*, old habits die hard. Sinful habits cling stubbornly. It is simply the nature of sin inherited from Adam rearing its head. It is the influence of the world we are born into before God translates us into His Kingdom of grace, peace, and joy—that we may be reconciled and dwell with Him, our Father.

It takes a continual, unending help from God to put the flesh to death. Our bodies aren't just sick from physical ailments; our minds are also sick with distractions, numbness, and perversions. Our hearts are diseased, and our souls are soiled. The way your mind wanders during prayers is a relatable example of this inward corruption.

Athanasius, in his book, *On the Incarnation*, explains this internal decay vividly, '*You must know, moreover, that the corruption which had set in was not external to the body but established within it. The need, therefore, was that life should cleave to it in corruption's place, so that, just as death was brought into being in the body, life also might be engendered in it.*'

Oh, how I wish I could take even a sip of whatever moves the elders[1] to fall perpetually on their faces before God! Thankfully, every believer will one day taste this fullness. In our new, incorruptible bodies, as citizens of Heaven, we will worship without distraction or weariness **(Philippians 3:21).**

If the twenty-four elders and heavenly beings never tire, then we will certainly never get weary of giving God undiluted worship without distractions or wandering thoughts. We will be single-minded in our adoration of Him just like they are **(Ezekiel 1:12, 20).**

Attention and proximity breed affection, and we can apply that to spiritual things, too. The elders who worship all day long do so because they see the One who is infinitely worthy to be praised. They are not mindless—they are moved. These beings have never known sin; they live in a reality that our earthly hearts struggle to fathom.

But for us, there is a better way.

---

1. Revelation 4:10–11.

7

WHAT IS THE POSSIBILITY?

In a world where everything changes in an instant, and 'certainty' becomes undone, where can we find hope?
—Maranatha

We have established that humanity's fallen state restrained us from being and living fully as God wanted. Sin made it impossible to walk by sight, for God was no longer perceivable due to the loss of spiritual sight—we could no longer look at God. This is the natural state of every human being born of Adam.

It seemed a hopeless, helpless situation—total alienation from the Father. Right? But only to man, for with God all things are possible according to His will, even though we might scarcely perceive them.

The tricky thing about sight is that we often only see

what we choose to focus on. When you read **Genesis 3**, what do you notice? Do you sigh at the curses on the serpent, Eve, and Adam? Do you shake your head at Eve's carelessness? Do you find yourself wishing, again and again, that she never ate that fruit while mulling over how much more *careful* and *discerning* you'd have been if you were in her shoes?

You are not the only one. But right there, smack in the middle of the curse, is the birth of hope. It is so small, so seemingly insignificant, like the proverbial mustard seed **(Matthew 17:20)**, that you might miss it if you are not careful. In fact, I have missed it many times myself; the blessing nestled so close to the curses!

> **Genesis 3:15 (KJV):**
> **And I will cause hostility between you and the woman, and between your offspring and her offspring.**
> **He will strike your head, and you will strike his heel.**

In theology, this verse is conceptualised as *protoevangelium*—the *first* Gospel. It introduces '*two elements previously unknown in the Garden of Eden, elements that are the basis of Christianity—the curse on mankind because of Adam's sin and God's provision for a Saviour from sin who would take the curse upon Himself.*'[1] The 'you' addressed in this verse is the serpent, the enemy who deceived Eve. The 'He' who would ultimately crush the serpent's head in victory is

1. Gotquestions.org: What is the protoevangelium?

Jesus Christ: the second Adam, our Saviour and Redeemer **(1 Corinthians 15:45).**

This is the possibility!

This is the Good News!

That Jesus, *God in the flesh*, was not a contingency plan in reaction to Satan's antics but in the prediction of them! He is the Lamb who was slain from the foundation of the world **(Revelation 13:8).** It is He who came to destroy the works of the devil **(1 John 3:8).**

Would you look at that?

The devil has always been playing a reactive, losing game. Redemption was not an improvisation; the sacrifice of Jesus was factored into the creation of the world. Before the Fall, before the serpent spoke, before humanity stumbled, Christ was already the answer.

What a comfort!

But we must remember that Adam and Eve had just sinned, setting in motion the degeneration of humanity. Though hope was announced right in the middle of the curse, its fulfilment would only come at God's appointed time. **Galatians 4:4 (NLT)** affirms the divine timing: '**... when the right time came, God sent his Son, born of a woman, subject to the law.**' Until that moment, Adam, Eve and indeed the entire human race would have to bear the brunt of their disobedience and rebellion. Yes, redemption was promised, but history would still have to run its painful course. We cannot separate God's mercy from His judgment. For it is precisely because God is inherently good that He must also be just, dispensing judgment where it is necessary. A God who overlooks sin would not be loving.

R.C. Sproul in *Saved from What* describes three characteristics of sin:

´There are three distinct ways in which human sin is described biblically. First, it is described as a debt, a failure to do what we are obligated to do. God as Creator has given us responsibilities for which He holds us accountable. If we do not carry out those responsibilities, we incur a debt.

Secondly, sin from the biblical perspective is an expression of enmity—a violation of the personal relationship that human beings are supposed to have with their Creator. When we sin against God, we break that relationship. We communicate not love or affection or devotion to our Creator, but a kind of hostility that has to be dealt with.

And thirdly, the Bible regards sin as a crime against God, an offense against His holiness, a transgression of His law.

If a crime has been committed, then we have to deal with penal sanctions. If a debt has been incurred, then payment must be made. If enmity has entered a personal relationship, if the relationship has been violated, that relationship must be restored.

Two questions I often encounter about sin and redemption are:

1. Why did God not send Christ immediately?
2. Why do we have to bear the curse of Adam when we had no part in his disobedience?

To answer the first question, God works according to His perfect timing for His good purpose **(Isaiah 60:22).**

There was a specific, appointed time for Christ to come to earth to fulfil His mission and redeem humanity. He came when the time was right. At the time when Adam and Eve had just sinned, the timing was not yet fulfilled. The Law had to be given, then history would follow its course, demonstrating humanity's need for a Saviour.

For the second question, God created humanity in such a way that one species, with its reproductive design, would propagate according to its kind. This means that whatever nature the first humans had would automatically be passed on to their offspring. The Bible records no children of Adam and Eve while they were in the Garden; only after their rebellion did they have descendants. Being prototype humans, every human born to these first sinners inherited a sinful nature. In theology, this principle is referred to as federal headship, where Adam, as the first man, acted as the representative of the human race, so his actions affected all his descendants.

Do you have birthmarks, physical traits or imperfections like your parents? You didn't exactly have a choice in the matter now, did you? In the same way, it may seem unfair, but Adam decided for all of us when he ate that fruit.

If you think about it, we have no right to salvation, let alone to dictate its timing. God did not owe it to us to save us. Christ is God's mercy in action! Even for those who lived before Jesus came in the flesh, Scripture makes it clear that none of us has an excuse, for God provided ways for the world to perceive Him—yet they did not **(Romans 1:18–20; Acts 14:17 & 17:26–28).**

About the timing, let us examine a hypothetical situation: say you are cooking a pot of yams, and you tell your younger sister not to go near the pot because it is hot and dangerous. You give her some fruit to eat and leave the kitchen to take a phone call. Upon your return, the pot is on the ground, its contents spilt, and your sister is crying, her hands burnt from touching the hot pot. She was so hungry she tried to check if the yams were done rather than make do with the fruit. But when you check, the yams still aren't ready. Would you serve half-cooked yams to your sister because of her desperation for them? Of course not. You would ensure it is done before giving it to her. This is the essence of timing.

In the meantime, your sister might sulk over her burnt fingers. She might also think you are withholding the yams out of anger or as punishment. Yet you know the truth: no matter how hungry she is, she must wait, because eating half-cooked yams is not an option. This is the essence of timing.

Imagine this, too: dinner is being prepared at home. The first son arrives just as the cooking begins. Two sisters come in halfway through, and the youngest enters the house as the meal is being served. Everybody will eat; however, those who arrived earlier had to wait. This is no perfect analogy, but it illustrates a truth we often miss: we are like the last-born child. We didn't have to endure the time before the Law. We didn't suffer the rigidity and impossibility that the Law imposed. We are not the generation that longed for the indwelling of the Holy Ghost or the ones that witnessed Jesus in the flesh, yet rejected Him. By God's grace, we live in an opportune moment in history, and we must take advantage of it.

The sacrifice of Jesus affects the past, present and future. Regardless of the generation, I believe everyone has had the opportunity to say yes to God. No one can stand before God with an excuse, for throughout the ages, He provided measures of grace and extended mercy, leaving signs so that people may seek Him and find Him.

Salvation was not strictly tied to the physical manifestation of Jesus. It has always been rooted in faith in God and belief in [His promise of] Christ. Abraham's faith in God's promise to make him a father of many nations **(Romans 4:18)** was credited to him as righteousness. Jesus had not yet come in the flesh, yet Abraham believed in Him and received salvation.

The promise to Abraham was not merely about fathering many children; it pointed to Christ. **Galatians 3:16 (NIV)** makes this clear: '**The promises were spoken to Abraham and to his seed. Scripture does not say "and to seeds," meaning many people, but "and to your seed," meaning one person, who is Christ.**' Through Christ, all who believe become children of Abraham, fulfilling God's promise to him and making him the father of countless nations—as innumerable as the stars! **(Genesis 15:5)**.

Jesus in **John 8:56 (NLT)** said of Abraham: '**Your father Abraham rejoiced as he looked forward to my coming. He saw it and was glad.**' The patriarchs of old believed in the Christ who was yet to come; we believe in the Christ who has come and is coming again!

Adam may have chosen for us the first time, but now

we have another opportunity. This is the possibility, our second chance; or in a way, our *first chance*—since Adam chose for us initially.

Have you chosen wisely?

How faithfully are you standing by your choice?

And if the choice still lies before you, will you make it now?

8

NOAH

I have often wondered why the miracle of the ark—wild animals dwelling alongside the domestic without turning them into prey—is not more widely told as one of God's great wonders. Perhaps, in that floating sanctuary, God was reminding creation of Eden: of what once was, and what could be again.

—Maranatha

The story of Noah was God's merciful attempt to cleanse the world and restore the *sanity* of *humanity*. (*Eyyy—see what I did there?*) After the first sin, the world entered a steady, accelerating, downward spiral. By the time we arrive at **Genesis 6**, Scripture gives us a sobering snapshot of just how far humanity had fallen.

Genesis 6:5–8 (NLT):
5 The Lord observed the extent of human wickedness on the earth, and he saw that everything they thought or imagined was consistently and totally evil.
6 So the Lord was sorry he had ever made them and put them on the earth. It broke his heart.
7 And the Lord said, "I will wipe this human race I have created from the face of the earth. Yes, and I will destroy every living thing—all the people, the large animals, the small animals that scurry along the ground, and even the birds of the sky. I am sorry I ever made them."
8 But Noah found favor with the Lord.

I USE THE WORD 'ATTEMPT' loosely, for God already knew what would happen. Yet, He didn't destroy the entire world like a potter would dissolve clay that refused to be moulded to his purpose. God sent a flood to nearly wipe out humanity as part of His gracious plan to remove impurity from already moulded clay without necessarily crushing the vessel.

Crushing the vessel would have been perfectly just, considering our act of high treason. Did we not commit cosmic treason against the Creator and King of the universe by choosing to rule over ourselves—His very own territory? Who vexes even an earthly king and leaves with his life? And which of us would hesitate to start over from scratch if the works of our hands refused to yield to our touch? But God, who is life, loves life.

Noah's faithfulness set him apart from the evil generation of his time. As the story unfolds, however, we see that even a righteous man cannot guarantee righteous offspring. A good man does not always produce good children, nor can he produce a sinless lineage, no matter how earnestly he desires to walk with God. Sin was the problem, not merely people. Therefore, sin itself had to be dealt with.

The flood resets the earth, but history quickly repeats itself. Right after the flood, Noah's son, Ham, made a mockery of his father's nakedness **(Genesis 9)**. This moment marked the beginning of Canaan's troubles, as Noah cursed Ham's lineage, declaring Canaan a servant to his relatives. Once again, sin began to spread through Noah's family. They could not help themselves.

Something to keep in mind is that many events before Jesus Christ pointed forward to Him. The flood, for example, represented both God's judgement and His mercy, as well as His unwavering commitment to the goodness of humanity. The ancient world had descended into chaos, and the flood became its annihilation. Noah warned the world of God's righteous judgement, yet not one person listened **(2 Peter 2:5)**.

Jesus Himself references Noah in the New Testament. In **Matthew 24:37–39 (NLT)**, He says, **'When the Son of Man returns, it will be like it was in Noah's day. In those days before the flood, the people were enjoying banquets and parties and weddings right up to the time Noah entered his boat. People didn't realize what was going to happen until the flood came and swept them**

all away. That is the way it will be when the Son of Man comes.'

Again, this is the problem of sin. At its core, sin is the rejection of God's Word—which reveals His ways—and the deliberate choice of self over Him.

Before the flood, in the story of Cain and Abel, the sons of Adam, God issues a warning to Cain immediately after rejecting his sacrifice. As a caring Father who desires to correct rather than condemn, God admonishes him in **Genesis 4:7 (NLT): 'You will be accepted if you do what is right. But if you refuse to do what is right, then watch out! Sin is crouching at the door, eager to control you. But you must subdue it and be its master.'**

God warns Cain of sin's malice, and His instruction —which applies not only to Cain but to every one of us —is that we *must* rule over sin. Sadly, we have sometimes left the doors of our hearts unguarded, allowing sin to move from its crouching at the door to sneak into our souls. Sin is that insidious guest who pretends it wants to stay for a week or two but arrives with three suitcases and a few friends. Then it never leaves and, before long, begins to order you about in your own house.

Cain fails at ruling over sin, and so does everyone else on earth. Yet faithful Noah finds favour with God. By this time, God was grieved by human wickedness and evil, regretting that He had made humanity in the first place. Thus, the decision to wipe the slate clean—to start over **(Genesis 6:5–8)**.

So many questions come to mind: Is the world more wicked now than it was then? (Yes, of course, because evil is progressive). Is God even more heartbroken now at human wickedness? Is there hope?

I'll say this: Noah demonstrates the power of one person's decision to follow God and the mercy God extends to those who love and fear Him. Time and again, the Bible shows how God accomplishes His purposes through one man's faithfulness: from preserving David's lineage despite Solomon's idolatry **(1 Kings 11:13)**, sparing Lot through the destruction of Sodom and Gomorrah for Abraham's sake **(Genesis 19)**, to repeatedly showing mercy on Israel because of Moses.

God chose to destroy the earth, a decision fully within His rights as Creator. However, Noah found favour in His eyes, and God set him apart for preservation. The flood came, cleansing the earth, and afterwards God established a covenant with Noah, a lasting confirmation of His faithfulness.

Genesis 8:20–21 (NLT):

20 Then Noah built an altar to the Lord, and there he sacrificed as burnt offerings the animals and birds that had been approved for that purpose.

21 And the Lord was pleased with the aroma of the sacrifice and said to himself, "I will never again curse the ground because of the human race, even though everything they think or imagine is bent toward evil from childhood. I will never again destroy all living things.

22 As long as the earth remains, there will be

planting and harvest, cold and heat, summer and winter, day and night.

Genesis 9:11–13 (NLT):
11 Yes, I am confirming my covenant with you. Never again will floodwaters kill all living creatures; never again will a flood destroy the earth.
12 Then God said, "I am giving you a sign of my covenant with you and with all living creatures, for all generations to come.
13 I have placed my rainbow in the clouds. It is the sign of my covenant with you and with all the earth."

I believe it is God's promise to Noah that has restrained the world from the full force of His judgement by flood. Otherwise, humanity might have faced a *purge* every now and then. Yes, the world may be even more wicked now than in Noah's time, but God never goes back on His Word.

Here is a glimpse of what it means for God to bind Himself to His Word.

Ezekiel 1:28 (NLT):
All around him was a glowing halo, like a rainbow shining in the clouds on a rainy day. This is what the glory of the Lord looked like to me.

Would you look at that?! God's throne, surrounded by

a rainbow, a vivid sign of His promise never to flood the earth again. Guzik[1] says in his commentary on Ezekiel:

> *'In John's heavenly vision, he saw the throne of God surrounded by a rainbow (Revelation 4:3). All around this setting of all sovereignty, power, authority and glory – this setting of the throne of God – God set a reminder of His promise to never destroy the earth again with water (Genesis 9:13-16), a promise that directs His sovereignty so that it is not capricious or against His promises.*
>
> *A throne says, "I can do whatever I want because I rule." A promise says, "I will fulfill this word to you, and I cannot do otherwise." A rainbow over the throne of God is a remarkable thing, showing that God will always limit Himself by His own promises.'*

What a comfort.
What a joy.

YET, this is not a reason for complacency, for Scripture reminds us that a time will come when '**... the heavens shall pass away with a great noise, and the elements shall melt with fervent heat, the earth also and the works that are therein shall be burned up' (2 Peter 3:10, KJV).**

But let us not rush ahead; we will come to that later. For now, here is where we stand: Noah happened, but

1. David Guzik's Enduring Word Bible Commentary on Ezekiel.

even a faithfulness like his did not give us the salvation our souls desperately needed.

What next?

9

THE LAW

To the law, I said, 'It's not you; it's me.'
—Maranatha

The subject of the Law can feel cumbersome, but we must grasp its gravity if we are to fully appreciate the lifting of the veil and the restoration of direct access to God once again, like in the Garden **(Matthew 27:51)**.

By the Law, I am referring specifically to the Ten Commandments, not the civil or ceremonial laws, given to the children of Israel. Even those civil and societal laws were fundamentally derived from the Ten Commandments. These Ten Commandments transcribed the character of God to fallen human beings who possessed the knowledge of good and evil but could scarcely tell their left from their right. For the knowledge of good and evil is not the wisdom to overcome evil.

By this point, we've come a long way from Noah—from Abraham, who received the promise, to Isaac, Jacob, and Joseph; to his brothers, who came to represent the twelve tribes of Israel; and finally to Israel's settlement, slavery and deliverance from Egypt.

What follows is the setting apart of the Israelites, God's chosen people, from the rest of the world.

It is important to note, however, that the people of Israel were not chosen because they were inherently special. Rather, they were chosen in the fulfilment of the promise (or covenant) God made to Abraham: to give him innumerable descendants and the land of Canaan (**Genesis 12:3 & 7; 17:4, 7, 8 & 21; 22:17; 26:24; 28:1–4 & 13**). God was not being partial in delivering these commands to the Israelites. He was simply keeping His promise to Abraham.

In **Exodus 4:22–23**, God refers to Israel as His first-born son. Once again, just as we saw with Noah, Abraham shows us how far-reaching the faithfulness of one man to God can be—its impact spilling beyond seasons, lifetimes, and generations yet unborn.

The Israelites were elected to receive God's promise, being of Abraham's chosen descendants; to no other nation did God reveal His laws and decrees (**Psalm 147:19–20**). **'Theirs is the adoption to sonship; theirs the divine glory, the covenants, the receiving of the law, the temple worship and the promises. Theirs are the patriarchs, and from them is traced the human ancestry of the**

Messiah, who is God over all, forever praised! Amen' (Romans 9:4–5).

All of these blessings and responsibilities were contained within the Law. Jesus Himself affirmed, '... **salvation is of the Jews' (John 4:22, KJV).**

Remember that by eating the forbidden fruit, every human gained the knowledge of good and evil, even though they rarely choose what is good. So, what was the purpose of the Law? These laws were a transcript of God's character, given to the Israelites as a means of setting them apart from the rest of humanity and teaching them —once again—how to be godly. The Law was given to Israel to show them how God desired them to live: loving Him, obeying Him, and walking in His ways.

The Law also revealed humanity's desperate need for a Saviour and pointed forward to the second Adam, Jesus Christ, who would also come from Abraham's lineage **(Galatians 3:29)**, and through whom we would become spiritual descendants and children of Abraham—thereby taking hold of the Promise too.

The Law, though spiritual **(Romans 7:14)**, was given to carnal, sinful people who promoted its misuse to suit their seared consciences. As we later see [in the case of the Pharisees], the Law was often taken to an extreme. Jesus, during His earthly ministry, rightly exegeted the Law, which had been grossly misinterpreted, misapplied and twisted into legalistic extremism. He did this not only in the Sermon on the Mount, amongst other teachings **(Matthew 5–7)**, but in the way He lived His life.

These misinterpretations given to the Law make the deadly nature of sin even more evident, for the children of

Israel had turned it into a hollow performance without soul—obedience in form, but not in humble fellowship with God.

Jesus corrected these false interpretations, showing that obeying the Law involves keeping both its inward and outward parts, not merely performing it for show.

> **Matthew 22:37–40 (CSB):**
> **37 He said to him, "Love the Lord your God with all your heart, with all your soul, and with all your mind.**
> **38 This is the greatest and most important command.**
> **39 The second is like it: Love your neighbor as yourself.**
> **40 All the Law and the Prophets depend on these two commands.**

But let us not sneer at the children of Israel. They could not perfectly keep the Law, nor can we, even in the twenty-first century, no matter how hard we try.

Why? The Law is spiritual, and humanity is carnal. The Law is a description of God's character. Think of it as love distilled into ten or more sentences. When we consider the fruit of God's Holy Spirit enumerated in **Galatians 5: 22–23 (KJV): love, joy, peace, longsuffering, gentleness, goodness, faith, meekness, temperance**, we find that '**AGAINST SUCH THERE IS NO LAW.**' This shows that the Law does not oppose this fruit of the Spirit. Were we to truly live in the Spirit, the Law would not be a burden, we would not struggle with covetousness, anger or greed.

There is no law *against* this fruit. Adam, before sin, possessed these traits naturally. The fallen man, however, became subject to the flesh, and thus needed the Law to reveal his sin and demonstrate the need for a Saviour. Fallen humanity is more predisposed to evil than good, and clearly, the Scripture says that we '**would not have known sin if it were not for the law. For example, I would not have known what it is to covet if the law had not said, Do not covet. And sin, seizing an opportunity through the commandment, produced in me coveting of every kind. For apart from the law, sin is dead' (Romans 7:7–8, CSB).**

The Law says, '*O sinner, can you keep me? Can you rise above your flesh and commit your ways to my rules? Can you abide by the holiness in my words*?' And the sinner tries again and again but fails, proving the undeniable need for a Redeemer. Without the Law, the depth of sin might remain unknown. In fact, it is precisely when the Law is made clear that the flesh rebels, craving nothing more than to go against it.

The Law proves our need for Jesus. Yet, without Him, nobody can keep the Law.

If the Law is truly a transcript of God's character, then it is perfect because the God who gave it is perfect. The problem arises when sinful people attempt to keep it; we simply cannot.

The sum of the Law has always been—and still is—love. Its purpose was to shape God's children into His likeness **(Matthew 5:45, Ephesians 5:1)**, to cultivate pure hearts by revealing sin, and to guide them towards a good and clear conscience **(1 Timothy 1:5).**

It is needless to point out again that the flesh never fails to put up resistance. Its power keeps us from fully yielding to God, stirring rebellion within us. Its guilt hinders repentance, further hardening our hearts and keeping us from turning back to God even when we know we have erred.

Romans 7:14, 22–23 (NLT):

14 So the trouble is not with the law, for it is spiritual and good. The trouble is with me, for I am all too human, a slave to sin.

22 I love God's law with all my heart.

23 But there is another power within me that is at war with my mind. This power makes me a slave to the sin that is still within me.

24 Oh, what a miserable person I am! Who will free me from this life that is dominated by sin and death?

25 Thank God! The answer is in Jesus Christ our Lord. So you see how it is: In my mind I really want to obey God's law, but because of my sinful nature I am a slave to sin.

Our answer, our salvation, is in Jesus Christ!

As the Law proved the need for a Saviour, it swiftly condemned its recipients when they failed to keep it. The Law revealed sin but offered no sustainable solution. It was a diagnosis and a prescription, but not for dead men with stony hearts. For even after the Israelites received it, they carried it out without good soul, their hearts and intentions being wicked.

> **Romans 3:20 (NLT):**
>
> **For no one can ever be made right with God by doing what the law commands. The law simply shows us how sinful we are.**

> **Isaiah 64:6 (NLT):**
>
> **We are all infected and impure with sin. When we display our righteous deeds, they are nothing but filthy rags.**
>
> **Like autumn leaves, we wither and fall, and our sins sweep us away like the wind.**

Nobody could keep the Law. And regardless of imperfect adherence to its tenets, it was still not enough to make us right with God. Apart from its diagnostic nature, there remained a pending debt over our heads—a consequence of sin that demanded payment.

The sacrifices offered in Israel of old were made per time/per sin, each one a temporary atonement. But picture being a pauper and owing a billionaire a large sum of money; you might sell off every organ in your body and still fall short. Yet, such an absurd scenario is even more conceivable than paying God back for our sins. His holy standard is impossible to attain because of our sinful nature. Attempting to keep the Law by the strength of the flesh only provokes self-righteousness (righteousness by works) which are paltry sums compared to the debt we owe. Talk about a proud pauper!

You can imagine the surprise of Jesus' audience in **Matthew 5** as He revealed the true meaning of the Law so different from what they had believed for generations, for how can murder begin from anger? Shock, disbelief, denial ... and, hopefully, acceptance—something like the infamous five stages of grief. The Law, in its full and true interpretation, was far too much for sinful humanity to keep. It still is, if we try to approach it apart from Jesus.

Jesus did not merely interpret the Law. Throughout His life, He demonstrated the elements of true humanity. The Ten Commandments are a transcript of God's character, fully displayed by Jesus, the perfect embodiment of the Law. He assured His followers:

Matthew 5:17–18 (MSG):
Don't suppose for a minute that I have come to demolish the Scriptures—either God's Law or the Prophets. I'm not here to demolish but to complete. I am going to put it all together, pull it all together in a vast panorama. God's Law is more real and lasting than the stars in the sky and the ground at your feet. Long after stars burn out and earth wears out, God's Law will be alive and working.

Jesus came to connect the dots, from the Law to His ultimate sacrifice, revealing the full picture of God's love for us, even from before Adam ate that fruit.

It is because of His righteousness, shared with us in

His death and resurrection, that we are no longer justified by the Law, but by putting our faith in Him. He is the fulfilment of the Law for all who believe in Him, and the living example of love and obedience we are called to follow.

> **2 Corinthians 5:21 (AMP):**
>
> **He made Christ who knew no sin to [judicially] be sin on our behalf, so that in Him we would become the righteousness of God [that is, we would be made acceptable to Him and placed in a right relationship with Him by His gracious lovingkindness].**

Hallelujah!

10

OT GOD VS NT GOD

Indeed, the same yesterday, today and forever, He IS.
—Maranatha

Are the *God of the Old Testament* and the *God of the New Testament* the same? The simple answer is 'yes' since Scripture affirms that God is unchanging; *'Jesus Christ is the same yesterday, today and forever'* **(Hebrews 13:8).**

But maybe we can go a little deeper.

The subject of salvation often provokes an attempt to reconcile the *Old Testament* Yahweh with the *New Testament* Jesus—a task many find difficult to embrace. While the tension may feel challenging, what is fatal is the belief that the Old and New Testaments represent two separate dispensations. They do not. The Bible is a single, complete narrative of God's plan to restore humanity, a story set in motion from Eden—this truth is a good place to start from.

So far, we have followed a trail from Adam to Noah, and from Abraham to Moses and the Law, to illustrate the entrance of sin and humanity's desperate need for a Saviour.

A saying I once heard in church put it concisely, '*The New is in the Old concealed, and the Old is in the New revealed.*'

The Old Testament presents us with types and shadows which, though easily overlooked, like **Genesis 3:15** (the *protoevangelium*), served as symbols and prophecies of what was to come. In the New Testament, God's plan comes into clearer view, as He chose *at that time* to reveal it fully through the incarnation of Jesus Christ.

Now, that God's plans were concealed at the time of the Old Testament does not mean that the people of that time were denied the opportunity to believe in the promise of salvation. Abraham, David, Noah—and maybe many more who may never have been recorded in Scripture—believed. They believed in what was to come; we believe in what has already come. Unlike them, we now possess a complete account of God's redemptive plan—*nothing missing, nothing contradictory*. Even so, I hold that God has always made room for salvation. He *is* the righteous judge, then, now and forever. He does not delight in the death of a sinner **(Ezekiel 18:23)**.

We also know, according to **Romans 2:11–16**, that God shows no favouritism. He judges those who receive the Law by the Law and those who did not receive the Law apart from the Law. What this means is that we are, again, without excuse before God **(Romans 1:20)**.

If a person in those times wasn't an Israelite, for example, and did not receive the Law as delivered by Moses, yet in their heart—like Cornelius in **Acts 10**—chose to do good according to their conscience (for every human is born with an awareness of good and evil), they would be justified by the Law because they had, in effect, conformed to it, even without knowing it. This is further proof that God values our actions over mere knowledge of His Word—our deeds must reflect our belief. And no, our works do not save us; yet, faith without works is dead **(James 2:26)**. For true saving faith is never alone.

God has always honoured humanity's free will by handing them over to the consequences of their choice, whether in ancient or modern times. This is why the Israelites could repeatedly turn away from God, face His punishment, and still be welcomed back when they genuinely repented—because God loves justice and mercy! Scratch that. God *is* justice and mercy. Just as He punished the heathen nations for idolatry and sin, so He also disciplined the Israelites when they strayed. No *ojoro*[1] . No cheating.

The Old Testament places great emphasis on holiness and the consequences for disobedience, which the New Testament, upon a cursory glance, seems to downplay because of grace. However, this is not a flaw in Scripture but a consequence of human [sinful] interpretation.

A consistent theme in the Old Testament seems to be

---

1. Nigerian colloquial expression which means to cheat or manipulate.

God's wrath *randomly* being poured on disobedient people. There are many examples, but I will focus on one to highlight a truth we cannot overlook, no matter how emotional the story might be.

In **2 Samuel 6:1–7**, God struck Uzzah dead for attempting to keep the Ark of the Covenant from falling. We might argue that Uzzah was trying to do a good thing, yet that is only a variable among constants, which are:

1. God had commanded that the Ark must not be touched, with death as the consequence **(Numbers 4:15)**. No matter how good certain actions may seem, disobedience to God's commands renders them wrong. Indeed, many instances of God punishing the Israelites were due to their disobedience and idolatry; judgement fully justified under the Old Covenant **(Deuteronomy 11:16–17; 26–28)**.

2. God is absolutely just and fair **(Deuteronomy 32:4; Psalm 89:14)**. If we believe that we serve a just God, we must recognise that every one of His actions is perfectly righteous, even when we do not fully understand His ways.

3. God sees the heart **(1 Samuel 16:7)**. All we know is that Uzzah tried to save the Ark, but we do not know what was in his heart that led him to act. If God, who sees the heart, deemed death the appropriate consequence, who are we, with

our spiritual impairment, to question His judgement? Let us not forget that, as sinners, our every inclination is tainted with sin—even our best intentions fall short before a holy God.

4. God is slow to anger **(Exodus 34:6)**. Something we often miss in this story is that King David did not follow God's instructions for transporting the Ark—they used a cart instead of having it carried on poles by the Levites. This disobedience was the underlying cause of Uzzah's death. Had they not used a cart, the oxen wouldn't have stumbled, and Uzzah would not have touched the Ark in violation of God's Law.

5. The Psalmist, under the Law, declares in Psalm 103 God's abundant mercy, reminding us that God does not punish us according to our sins. If He did, who could survive? In **2 Samuel 24:14**, after sinning, David pleads to fall into the hands of God, rather than men, because He could trust in the Lord's mercies. Even now, God remains patient with all, for His kindness is meant to lead us to repentance. As sin increases, so does His grace! **(Romans 2:4 & 5:20; 2 Peter 3:9)**.

6. The point? God's wrath often comes after a long period of patience and mercy. Even when

David initially disobeyed by transporting the Ark wrongly, God showed mercy. Yet for a holy object like the Ark, the consequences were far more severe. I believe that Uzzah was a casualty of King David's disobedience.

7. God *is* the potter **(Isaiah 64:8)**. He alone reserves the right to give and take life as He pleases, for all life belongs to Him. This might seem harsh, yet the truth that He is love tempers it. He is neither unjust nor unkind. He is justice and mercy. He is God.

GOD HAS NOT CHANGED. I daresay that He was far more patient with the Israelites and the people of the Old Testament than we often care to admit. **Romans 3:25 (NLT)** declares, **'For God presented Jesus as the sacrifice for sin. People are made right with God when they believe that Jesus sacrificed his life, shedding his blood. This sacrifice shows that God was being fair WHEN HE HELD BACK and did not punish those who sinned in times past.'**

The Lord actually *held back*! The Israelites witnessed the mighty hand of God time and again, and yet they murmured and disobeyed Him so many times with an audacity I cannot place a finger on. *(Oh, wait ... please, pardon my self-righteous anger. I just realised that my description of the Israelites also applied to me when I was in my sin—if not now as well. Oops. I digress).*

The Israelites had a system of atonement in place, and even though it was only a shadow of what was to come in Jesus, we must see that even the Law was an expression of God's mercy to them as much as a good conscience was His mercy to the Gentiles without the Law (consider, for example, Nineveh accepting Jonah's message). Using the former analogy of a dinner being prepared, we might liken the Israelites to the child who arrived first.

Now, here's another thing you might have missed in the Scripture above, **'God PRESENTED Jesus as the sacrifice for sin.'**

R.C. Sproul, in his book *Saved from What*, clarifies salvation in clearer, modern terms:

> *'At the core of the biblical message of salvation is another concept often obscured in modern thought. Salvation is of the Lord. No human being has the resources, the power, the money, or the merit to save himself. The necessary power for rescue is not in us. It must come from God. Salvation is of the Lord because only the Lord can accomplish it.*
>
> *Salvation is of the Lord, we tend to forget that salvation is also from the Lord. What do we need to be saved from? We need to be saved from God—The last thing in the world the impertinent sinner ever wants to meet on the other side of the grave is God. But the glory of the gospel is that the One from whom we need to be saved is the very One who saves us. God in saving us saves us from Himself. Woe unto those who have no Saviour on the day of wrath.*
>
> *When we consider that we deserve to be consumed by His fury and realize that His fury has instead consumed Jesus in our place, when we recognize the greatness of the peril, we then are able to see the greatness of the salvation that He has*

> *bestowed upon us. How shall we escape if we neglect so great a salvation?'*

Remember **John 3:16**? God *gave* His Son! As explained in previous chapters, sin is a violation of God's commands, placing us in debt and enmity with Him. Because we have sinned and fallen short of His holy standard, He is the offended party. He never broke a promise or betrayed us; we did. This means that it is ultimately His prerogative to determine the acceptable atonement for our offence.

Consider this analogy: a driver crashes into your fence. A simple 'sorry' might suffice if it were merely a case of a stranger stepping on your foot by mistake, but not here, because real injury has been done and damages incurred. It is up to you to press charges or let the offender off. In the same way, it is up to God, the One we have offended, to determine what will atone for the debt we have accrued. He is the one we truly owe for our act of cosmic treason.

We might never have an incident like Uzzah's again, since holy items like the Ark of the Covenant are no longer needed as God does not dwell in temples made with human hands **(Acts 7:48)**.

However, the wages of sin is still death.

In His mercy, God exchanged our death for life by presenting Jesus as a *forever* atonement for us! God is not the 'bad cop' while Jesus is the 'good cop'. Jesus did not *plead* with God to accept His sacrifice so we could escape punishment. Nor was His life taken from Him, for He laid it down of His own volition **(John 10:18)**. The Godhead is united in their love for mankind!

Constantly searching for loopholes in the Old Testament to accuse God of injustice rather than seeking to understand what the Word *really* teaches may reveal more about the state of one's own heart than about God. God has not changed. Believe that.

Both the Old and New Testaments emphasise God's holiness and the call to love Him with our hearts, minds, and bodies. Yet, unlike the Old Testament, the New Testament provides us with an *added help*: God, in His generosity and mercy, has given us the Holy Spirit, a constant Helper, to guide us in obeying His laws after the death and resurrection of Jesus.

Therefore, this is the natural progression of the story:

> **We are born in sin → The Law is given to reveal our sin and our desperate need for salvation → We cannot obey the Law; we try and we fail → Along comes Jesus: His sacrifice redeems us, His blood breaks the yoke of sin and death, His love softens our hearts and we receive the Holy Spirit → Now, empowered by Him, we can return to the holy commandments and truly keep all ten of them!**

Hear the Lord Jesus when He says, '**Think not that I am come to destroy the law, or the prophets: I am not come to destroy, but to fulfil' (Matthew 5:17, KJV).** None of the Ten Commandments, hard to obey as they may be, has been nullified by His coming. Jesus came to fulfil them and show us *how* to keep them!

So, we do not stop at just the forgiveness of our sins. The Bible clearly says, '**Shall we continue in sin, that**

grace may abound?' (Romans 6:1, KJV). If we stop at God's forgiveness without embracing the ability His grace gives us to rise above sin and obey the Law, we cut short this beautiful story of salvation.

When Jesus was crucified, the temple's veil was torn **(Matthew 27:51)**. The temple symbolised God's presence, which, before that moment, could only be accessed by the priests through a rigorous process of cleansing and other rituals. With the veil torn, even we Gentiles, once given over to idolatry, now have access to God—a God we did not know before!

ATHANASIUS, in *On the Incarnation*, puts it this way:

> *'But now all over the world men are forsaking the fear of idols and taking refuge with Christ; and by worshipping Him as God they come through Him to know the Father also, Whom formerly they did not know. He has persuaded not only those close at hand, but literally the entire world to worship one and the same Lord and through Him the Father.'*

Neither Jews nor Gentiles need anyone to mediate access to God. Through Jesus, we can now come directly to Him.

But this raises important questions:

How does the sacrifice of Jesus even make sense?

Why did it have to be Him?

Who is this Jesus?

CONFORMITY

11

THE ROAD TO PERFECTION

Walking in His steps. These shoes seem too big to fill, but I will try. His Spirit is here!
—Maranatha

I began this narration with the creation story to offer a glimpse into the original order of things and how God designed life to be for every person who would one day walk the earth.

Intimacy, unbroken fellowship, and a life without sin; with these relics of the past, we can look into the future and decipher what it holds, by God's grace. We can hope.

Our beings writhe under the weight of earthly brokenness. We long for something beyond this world, something that feels just out of reach. And so, we often turn our gaze upward, seeking something ethereally soothing when the world fails us, as it so often does.

In **Matthew 6**, we observe a stark difference between the heaven we long for and the earth on which we live. On earth we pray to God, '**Thy kingdom come, Thy will be done in earth, as it is in heaven' (Matthew 6:10, KJV).** In Heaven, where God's throne sits, His will is always done. We sometimes struggle to put on our worship hats for morning devotion, while the twenty-four elders in Heaven can hardly restrain themselves from falling in worship of the One who sits on the throne **(Revelation 4:10–11).**

Coming from a sinful heritage, Heaven may seem very far away, yet by God's grace, it is not only when we die that we enter it. In His unfathomable, unconditional love for His image-bearers, God made a way to ensure that we can experience Heaven—not when our time on earth is done, and we reach some distant place above—but the moment we get to a specific decision: Him. He is the common factor in Heaven and on earth. He is what makes Heaven so special, for when we long for Heaven, it is God we are really longing for.

How do we get there? Every destination needs a path, and for Heaven, that path is the Narrow Way—Jesus. Born of a virgin and fully human, like you and me, yet fully God. He came to ensure our redemption, the full payment of our debt, and the rekindling of our resemblance to our heavenly Father.

> **Here is the progression of events, once more:** We are born in sin → The Law is given to reveal our sin and our desperate need for salvation → We cannot obey the Law; we try and we fail → Along comes Jesus: His sacrifice redeems us, His blood breaks the yoke of sin and death,

His love softens our hearts and we receive the Holy Spirit → Now, empowered by Him, we can return to the holy commandments and truly keep all ten of them!

Jesus, who is God in the flesh, came to save us from our sin. Sin is severally described in the Bible **(Matthew 6:12)** as a debt that needs to be paid because the heavens and the earth are built on principles ordained by God, and when a person does *'anything that tends not to glorify God, he contracts a debt with Divine Justice.'* [1]

How exactly does a human pay God back? We cannot. He pays Himself back by Himself, on our behalf.

Isaiah 59:16–17, 20 (AMP) clarifies:

He saw that there was no man, and was amazed that there was no one to intercede [on behalf of truth and right]; Therefore His own arm brought salvation to Him, And His own righteousness sustained Him.

For He [the Lord] put on righteousness like a coat of armor, and salvation like a helmet on His head; He put on garments of vengeance for clothing And covered Himself with zeal [and great love for His people] as a cloak.

1. The Adam Clarke Commentary: Commentary on Matthew 6 by Adam Clarke.

> **"A Redeemer (Messiah) will come to Zion, and to those in Jacob (Israel) who turn from transgression (sin)," declares the Lord.**

Jesus, our Messiah, was the only acceptable and sufficient sacrifice. Only God can pay a God-sized debt, so He did—in Christ, and for all time. Recall that since God is the offended party, only He could decide what would suffice to atone for humanity's sins.

To forgive us, Jesus Christ had to die for our sins. Somehow, it is the sweetest and scariest thing I have ever heard: He knew we would not be able to help ourselves, so He already made provisions to do so.

You know, many times, I hear people insinuate that certain things are for 'Christians' and that what we believe applies solely to the Christian faith. But a person believing that they randomly fell from the sky does not erase the reality that they were incubated in their mother's womb and delivered after nine months or so. Likewise, choosing to believe there is no God despite the abundance of evidence does not remove the presence of God from earth, even if that person decides to be blind to it.

God's original order: intimacy, unbroken fellowship with Him, and a life without sin, is meant not for Christians alone but for everyone who will believe in His Name.

The reality is that we are all made in the image and likeness of God. At the same time, we are all fallen; sinners by *original* nature inherited from Adam. The devil does not need to appear to each of us as he did to Eve. All he needed was an inroad of sin through the first man, passed on to all humanity, which is why he now has our own flesh working against us to his advantage **(Romans 7).**

Our only way out is a Saviour who will reconcile us, the children, with God the Father, restoring His image and likeness in us, as it was in the beginning. And this is not by '**...works of righteousness which we have done, but according to his mercy he saved us, by the washing of regeneration, and renewing of the Holy Ghost; Which he shed on us abundantly through Jesus Christ our Saviour; That being justified by his grace, we should be made heirs according to the hope of eternal life'** (Titus 3:5–7, KJV).

Ephesians 4: 22–24 (CSB) says:
22 to take off your former way of life, the old self that is corrupted by deceitful desires,
23 to be renewed in the spirit of your minds,
24 and to put on the new self, the one created according to God's likeness in righteousness and purity of the truth.

If we are to put on the new self in God's likeness, then the old self is not in His likeness. In fact, perhaps this new self is only new to us, but to God it is merely the way things should have always been. After all, a child should resemble their father!

The key to unlocking our resemblance to our Father is Jesus. How? '**If you openly declare that Jesus is Lord and believe in your heart that God raised him from the dead, you WILL be SAVED. For it is by believing in your heart that you are MADE RIGHT with God, and it is by**

openly declaring your faith that you are saved' (Romans 10:9–10, NLT).

When our bodies are contaminated, we purge. In the same way, we must be cleansed from sin—confessing our sins and partaking of what [who] will heal the impurity of our souls.

The road to perfection, to Heaven on earth, to God, is Jesus. Through Him, **'God has shown us a way to be made right with him without keeping the requirements of the law, as was promised in the writings of Moses and the prophets long ago. We are made right with God by placing our faith in Jesus Christ. And this is true for everyone who believes, no matter who we are' (Romans 3:21–22, NLT).**

Why couldn't God just forgive us all, since He is God? Well, would you trust a God who does not keep His own Word? Our belief in [and reverence for] God is rooted in His infallibility and uncompromising holiness. Without His justice, sin would run unchecked, and there would be no reward for obedience or good works.

For every act of disobedience, there must be a corresponding penalty. Judgement must be passed, and payment—a compensation in place of the crime committed—must be made.

So, God could not help but be just. Yet, He also could not help but be merciful. Though animals were used as temporary payment, they were not sustainable; hence, Christ. Once and for all. God's justice required punishment, but His mercy demanded salvation. These met in perfect harmony on the cross of Calvary when Jesus

Christ, on our behalf, bore the fullness of God's wrath, satisfying God's justice and redeeming us from sin!

We could not perfectly keep the Law, but we were never meant to. Our hearts are not inclined to do what is right **(Jeremiah 17:9)** because of sin. It is for this reason that Jesus is the only way to soften our stony hearts. He is the Gospel, the Good News—the rope God threw down to pull us out of the pit of sin. He is God's *trump card* against the kingdom of darkness, and the means by which He continually woos sinful people.

Who, then, is this Jesus?

12

WHO IS THIS JESUS?

He makes the darkness tremble. Our Prince of Peace.
—Maranatha

I once heard it said that your answer to the question, '*Who is God?*'[1] is the most important thing about you. I find that statement has a ring of truth to it. Your answer could be a culmination of all that God has revealed of Himself to you. Sometimes, it may be influenced by the testimonies and opinions of others [though external influences should always be carefully sifted and tested].

In a conversation with a friend, she spoke of how she had seen God in many ways throughout her life, but never

1. A. W. Tozer, in *The Knowledge of the Holy*, says, '*What comes into our minds when we think about God is the most important thing about us.*'

as her provider. At first, I did not understand her statement, but as she continued, it brought some clarity, and I reflected on how this might be a common experience among many Christians. She meant that, having always had alternate forms of security—her jobs, for instance—she had never faced a situation where her only source of provision was God. As a result, she had not known Him intimately as her Provider.

We can know God in one way and not know Him in another, even though He is all things.

Who is Jesus to you? In **Matthew 16:13–20**, Jesus asked his disciples about His identity. Initially, they gave a generic answer, but Jesus pressed further, and Peter responded with a truth born of conviction from God, perhaps confirmed by his personal experiences with Jesus. One such encounter is the fishing experience recorded in **Luke 5:1–11**, which gives context to Peter's declaration, **'You are the Messiah, the Son of the living God'.**

Our understanding of Jesus often begins with the testimony of others, such as with the Samaritan woman in **John 4**, or through Scripture, and gradually deepens as we encounter Him personally and form our own convictions.

Colossians 1:13–14 (NLT) says, **'For he has rescued us from the kingdom of darkness and transferred us into the Kingdom of his dear Son, who purchased our freedom and forgave our sins.'** This dear Son is Jesus, the One who purchased our freedom and delivered us from the bondage of our disobedience.

. . .

Verses 16–17 provide even more context; here, we see Jesus' role in the creation story of Genesis.

> **16 for through him God created everything in the heavenly realms and on earth. He made the things we can see and the things we can't see—such as thrones, kingdoms, rulers, and authorities in the unseen world. Everything was created through him and for him.**
> **17 He existed before anything else, and he holds all creation together.**

When God said **'Let us …'** at the beginning **(Genesis 1:26)**, He was referring to the Godhead (or Trinity) comprising God the Father, Jesus the Son and the Holy Spirit. Jesus is God.

For most people, our primary introduction to the person of Jesus Christ comes in **John 3:16–17**, and what a fitting Scripture that is. It captures the depth of God's love, the actions that prove that love, and the results of it for us. The **NLT** puts it this way:

> **16 For this is how God loved the world: He gave his one and only Son, so that everyone who believes in him will not perish but have eternal life.**
> **17 God sent his Son into the world not to judge the world, but to save the world through him.**

God sent Jesus to save the world! To save you and me

from sin. Through Christ, God reconciled the world to Himself.

> **For God was in Christ, reconciling the world to himself, no longer counting people's sins against them. For God made Christ, who never sinned, to be the offering for our sin, so that we could be made right with God through Christ (2 Corinthians 5:19 & 21, NLT).**

In teaching His disciples about forgiveness, Jesus told us the story of the Unforgiving Servant in **Matthew 18:21–35.** In this parable, the servant owed his master a debt he could not pay. Settling it would require that **'he, his wife, his children, and everything he had be sold,'** and even then, it might not cover the loss his master suffered. Just like the master in the story, God cleared our debt by sending Jesus to purchase our freedom with His blood. Though we are born of Adam, through faith we are born [again] of Christ **(John 3:5–6).**

Jesus bought our freedom with His blood for without the shedding of blood, there is no forgiveness of sins **(Hebrews 9:22).** Under God's Law, the Old Testament high priest, acting as a mediator between God and the people, was required to offer sacrifices for himself first, as a sinful human born of Adam, before offering sacrifices for the people.

These sacrifices consisted of unblemished animals, whose blood appeased for the sins of the people, but only for a time; which is why they had to be offered over and again as the people kept sinning. But with Jesus, His sacrifice was once and for all, covering all sins past, present and future **(Hebrews 10:10; Romans 6:10).**

Jesus was without sin **(2 Corinthians 5:21)** and therefore did not need to offer a sacrifice for Himself. It was His very sinlessness, as God, that qualified Him to atone for the sinful. As our High Priest, His pure blood, infinitely more excellent than the blood of any unblemished animal, was shed not for Himself but for us! For only perfect righteousness can atone for sin.

> **Hebrews 9:12–14 (CSB)** explains:
>
> **12 he entered the most holy place once for all time, not by the blood of goats and calves, but by his own blood, having obtained eternal redemption.**
>
> **13 For if the blood of goats and bulls and the ashes of a young cow, sprinkling those who are defiled, sanctify for the purification of the flesh,**
>
> **14 how much more will the blood of Christ, who through the eternal Spirit offered himself without blemish to God, cleanse our consciences from dead works so that we can serve the living God?**

From the time when the Ten Commandments were given till now, we have been unable to keep God's Law because of our inherited sinful nature. This struggle is evident in our daily lives, where we often know what is right yet do otherwise.

Jesus changed this because, through His sacrifice, He conquered sin and all that accompanied it: death, guilt, shame, powerlessness, helplessness over sin, etc.

Through Christ's sacrifice, **'the just requirement of**

the law would be fully satisfied for us, who no longer follow our sinful nature but instead follow the Spirit' (Romans 8:4, NLT). This means that by Christ, we are empowered to keep the Law through His Spirit, which now dwells in us, for having accepted Jesus as our Saviour, we are justified before God and freed from the dominion of sin **(Romans 5:1).**

Jesus Christ is the fulfilment of the Law. In **Matthew 5:17**, He makes it clear that He did not come to abolish the Law of Moses, but to bring a complete understanding, heart, and transformation into it, as His sermons in **Matthew 5–7** demonstrate. Beyond this, Jesus adds something no one else could ever boast of: untainted humanity achieved through His conception by the Virgin Mary through the power of the Holy Ghost!

The sacrifice of Jesus—His death and resurrection—carries profound implications for you and me:

First, we are saved from our sins through faith in Jesus' purchase of blood; we no longer owe a debt but are now reconciled with God, our Father, just as it was meant to be from the beginning. Jesus bore the full weight and consequences of our sins, burdens that once crushed us, so that we could receive God's blessings and peace **(Isaiah 53:4–5; Matthew 11:28–30).**

See how Spurgeon describes this in connection with **Zechariah 13:7:**

> *'... One of our Lord's servants ... pictured a storm gathering in the heavens. The darkness was deepening, and soon came the thunder and lightning, and the storm shook the earth. He saw before him a towering mountain, with its peak lifted high*

> *toward heaven. At the foot of it lay a small, sheltered settlement. The storm seemed all concentrated around the mountain's brow that was the center of the battle of the elements. That lofty peak seemed to be split and broken to shivers by the dread artillery of God. The settlement down below was in comparative peace—only some gentle drops of rain fell on it, fertilizing its fields. And he who gave the illustration said, "That peak was the Christ of God, Jesus the substitute and security of his people, standing in our place, on whom burst the full storm of Jehovah's wrath that the soft drops of pity and of grace might fall on the people for whom he suffered."*

Second, in Jesus is the unity of all humanity. Unlike before, when the Jews were singled out for salvation, Jesus has now brought together all races, both Jews and Gentiles alike, with the Gentiles abandoning their gods to bow at His feet **(Ephesians 2:12–14).**

Third, we are saved from spiritual and eternal death through the sacrifice of Jesus. Just as He died and rose again, conquering death, we die to our sins and rise again by believing in Him and receiving new life—the perfection of which we will experience when He returns for us at His Second Coming. The eternal life we receive begins the moment we accept Jesus, not merely at physical death **(1 Corinthians 15:42–57; Luke 17:21; Revelation 1:5).**

Fourth, through Jesus we regain our access to God **(Ephesians 2:13, 18)**, a privilege lost through Adam's sin—and it is no small privilege to address God as Father **(1 John 3:1).** The intimate relationship meant to exist between a Father and His children has been restored! Without Christ, we cannot stand before God, because He is holy and cannot tolerate sin. But by believing in Jesus and accepting His payment for our debt, God now sees us through the precious blood of His Son and carries us into His embrace, forgiving our sins and blotting out our transgressions. At Jesus' death, the temple's veil was split into two **(Matthew 27:51)**, symbolising that all children of God now have direct access to a place once reserved only for the high priest.

Fifth, through Jesus, we gain the power to know and internalise God's Law, which is now written in our hearts **(Hebrews 10:21–22)**. It is this power that allows us to know Him intimately and reflect His love to all around us. The Old Testament prophecies about a time when the Law would be within, not merely external, point to Jesus. For example, **Jeremiah 31:34 (KJV)** says, **'And they shall teach no more every man his neighbour, and every man his brother, saying, Know the Lord: for they shall all know me, from the least of them unto the greatest of them, saith the Lord: for I will forgive their iniquity, and I will remember their sin no more.'** We must remember, however, that we do not actually *keep* the Law perfectly in ourselves, in the sense that we are sinless and can now perfectly satisfy its requirements **(1 John 1:8–9)**. Rather, it is Jesus, our Mediator, who has fully fulfilled the Law, and it is His perfection that is credited to us when we believe.

Sixth, through Jesus' finished work on the cross, we are justified by God's grace. This does not mean that Christians are perfect, as is often expected, but that we are imputed the righteousness of One who is perfectly righteous—Jesus. In the Old Testament, unblemished animals were sacrificed for the forgiveness of the sins of the people, but these sacrifices were only temporary. With Jesus, we are credited with His righteousness, which is eternal! It is this righteousness that allows sinful people like you and me to stand before a holy God and call Him our Father. As is said in **Hebrews 10:14 (KJV): 'For by one offering he hath perfected for ever them that are sanctified.'** This was a perfect sacrifice, offered by a perfect Person, to perfect imperfect people.

Seventh, the sacrifice of Jesus is the only way we gain dominion over the world—over sin, evil, and death—which once kept us captive. In Christ, we exercise this dominion through our sonship in God **(Romans 8:14–17; Ephesians 2:6)**, for everything has been subjected under Jesus Christ by His victory on the cross **(Ephesians 1:22)**. Christ secured this dominion through sacrifice, and we access it by faith in what He has accomplished for us.

Eighth, we become children again, and God dwells in us **(Romans 8:15–17; Ephesians 2:22)**. Children naturally want to imitate everything their parents do. While this tendency may wane as they grow, in the Kingdom of God —which is countercultural **(Romans 12:2)**—our dependence on God does not diminish but increases as we mature in Him.

Ninth, through Jesus, we gain a Shepherd who guides us in the way of God **(John 10:27–29)**, rather than following the paths of men in which we were once led—and factually misled **(Matthew 9:36)**.

Finally, through Jesus we become partakers of the divine nature; we get to look more and more like God! **2 Peter 1:4 (ESV)** says it is through His divine power that, **'… he has granted to us his precious and very great**

promises, so that through them you may become partakers of the divine nature, having escaped from the corruption that is in the world because of sinful desire.'

> Athanasius, in *On the Incarnation,* describes it in this way:
>
> *'His being in creation does not mean that He shares its nature; on the contrary, all created things partake of His power.'*

All these are possible through faith in Jesus. As **John 3:16** affirms, whoever *believes* in Jesus will not perish but have everlasting life. And make no mistake, Jesus is not passive about our redemption. As He says in **John 10:15, 17–18 (ESV): "just as the Father knows me and I know the Father; and I lay down my life for the sheep. For this reason the Father loves me, because I lay down my life that I may take it up again. NO ONE TAKES IT FROM ME, but I lay it down of my own accord. I have authority to lay it down, and I have authority to take it up again. This charge I have received from my Father."'**

Kathy Keller, in *The Meaning of Marriage*, describes it beautifully: '*... it was not an assault on the dignity and divinity (but rather led to the greater glory) of the Second Person of the Godhead to submit himself, and assume the role of a servant ... The Son submits to the Father's headship with free, voluntary, and joyful eagerness, not out of coercion or inferiority.*'

Jesus is our first *actual* encounter with the identity of God, for He leads the way to the Father **(John 14:6).** In the Old Testament, the Israelites had a veiled glimpse of God, mediated through Moses, who bore the Ten Commandments. When Moses spoke to the Israelites about the Law, they could not look upon his face, which shone so brightly, reflecting the glory of God, so he had to wear a veil **(Exodus 34:34–35)**.

To understand the concept of a veil, consider its purpose—it hides or covers. Imagine putting on sunglasses to protect your eyes from the sun. What happens? Even the sun, brightly shining, becomes dim, and you can look at it, something you could not do before.

In the same way, the Israelites, recipients of the Old Covenant, put on figurative *Ray-Bans* not even to interact with God directly, but to listen to His lowly messenger, Moses, and this dimmed their perception of Him in no small way. For though Moses was the one wearing the veil, it was their sight that was subdued. The New Testament also gives additional insight into how a *veil* covers the heart of whoever listens to Moses, representative of the Law and the Old Covenant **(2 Corinthians 3:13–16)**. The veiling was two-fold!

Guess what? Even though Moses, known to be a friend of God, removed the veil when he went into the presence of God, God, out of love, did not allow him to look at His face **(Exodus 33:20)**. This means that the reflection on Moses' face, which made the Israelites fearful, was a diminished glory. But in Jesus, we get to look upon the face of our God, our Father and King—and not just physically but spiritually—for it is the very coming of Christ that allows us to more fully perceive and understand God.

With Jesus, we encounter the true identity of God. When we turn to Christ, the veil is removed—the Old

Covenant with its fading glory is set aside, and a new, better covenant takes its place **(Hebrews 10:20; 2 Corinthians 3:16; Hebrews 8:7–9)**.

Unlike Moses, too, we don't have to encounter just God's back. **Colossians 1:15 (AMP)** says that Jesus is the **'exact living image [the essential manifestation] of the unseen God [the visible representation of the invisible], the firstborn [the preeminent one, the sovereign, and the originator] of all creation.'** This image of God, visible in Jesus, is not merely physical; otherwise, nobody after the death and resurrection of Jesus could ever behold God. Rather, Jesus reveals God's character—preserving His testament for us now—and we can more clearly recognise His presence because, this time, He came as a man, just like us!

Fully God and Fully Man

Why did Jesus, God the Son, have to come as a man to die for our sins? Since man sinned, the requirements for atonement had to be borne by a man **(Hebrews 2:14–15).** Yet, only God could bear the consequence of our sins — the great wrath of God—and not be eternally destroyed.

> *'The object or thing which Christ gave for a ransom was Himself, not His body alone, nor His body and soul only, but His person consisting of His two natures, human and divine.*
>
> *Question: How could His divine nature be given up? Could it suffer? Could it die?*
>
> *Answer: First, the Deity simply considered in and by itself, could not die. For the Son of God assumed a human*

> *nature into the unity of His divine nature, uniting them together "without confusion, change, division, or separation," in one person. That which is done by one nature is done by the person, and in that respect the Scripture often attributes it to the other nature, as when it is said that they "crucified the Lord of glory" (1 Cor. 2:8) and God purchased the church "with his own blood" (Acts 20:28). Second, though the divine nature of Christ did not suffer, it did support the human nature, and added dignity, worth, and efficacy to the sufferings of that nature. Third, Christ's divine nature had proper and particular works in the work of redemption, as to sanctify His human nature, to take away our sins, to reconcile us to God, and the like.'*
>
> —William Gouge in *Building a Godly Home, Volume 1: A Holy Vision for Family Life*

Jesus *is* God, which is why He could come to die for us. In His human nature, Jesus completely fulfilled the righteous demands of God to save us. He bore the burden of God's wrath upon His human nature through the power of His deity, just as only a skilled teacher can teach a student accurately—can another man, also drowning in sin, save his brethren from sin? **(Hebrews 7:26).**

Furthermore, in any fight, quarrel or disagreement between two parties, it stands to reason that a mediator has stakes on both sides. Otherwise, the mediator risks being perceived as biased when a conclusion is reached.

Jesus had stakes on both sides; being fully God, He understood the gravity of sin and the dire cost it demanded, and being fully man also, He understood the plight of humanity and its helplessness in the struggle against sin.

As **1 Timothy 2:5** tells us, Jesus is the only mediator between God and mankind. A mediator's role is to help two parties in disagreement find common ground and bring about reconciliation. Athanasius, in *On the Incarnation*, writes:

> *'Thus He ensured that men should recognize Him in the part who could not do so in the whole, and that those who could not lift their eyes to His unseen power and yet did not behold Him but remained in sin might recognize and behold Him in the likeness of themselves. For, being men, they would naturally learn to know His Father more quickly and directly by means of a body that corresponded to their own and by the Divine works done through it; for by comparing His works with their own they would judge His to be not human but Divine.*
>
> *As, then, he who desires to see God Who by nature is invisible and not to be beheld, may yet perceive and know Him through His works, so too let him who does not see Christ with his understanding at least consider Him in His bodily works and test whether they be of man or God. If they be of man, then let him scoff; but if they be of God, let him not mock at things which are no fit subject for scorn, but rather let him recognize the fact and marvel that things divine have been revealed to us by such humble means, that through death deathlessness has been made known to us, and through the Incarnation of the Word the Mind whence all things proceed has been declared, and its Agent and Ordainer, the*

> *Word of God Himself. He, indeed, assumed humanity that we might become God.'*

Reaching an agreement often requires compromise or sacrifice. For God, that sacrifice was made in the person of Jesus, who paid the debt we owed. Our response, then, is a sacrifice of our own: the surrender of our stubborn flesh —our will—to the Lord Jesus, by believing in and trusting in the payment He has already made.

Commenting on the seventh beatitude—**'Blessed are the peacemakers, for they will be called sons of God' (Matthew 5:9, CSB)**—Spurgeon[2] likens the ministry of peacemakers to that of Jesus. He writes:

> *'And he sometimes putteth himself between the two, when they are very angry, and taketh the blows from both sides, for he knows that* **so Jesus did**, *who took the blows from his Father and from us also, that so by suffering in our stead, peace might be made between God and man.'*

Think back to that chasm that separated the rich man from Lazarus **(Luke 16:19–31)**. The rich man, now in torment in Hades, asked for water to cool his tongue, and Lazarus, now in Abraham's bosom, replied: '**... between us and you a great chasm has been set in place, so that those who want to go from here to you cannot, nor can anyone cross over from there to us.**' This is such a chasm that only Christ can span. Only on Christ's wings can the

2. Quoted in David Guzik's Enduring Word Bible Commentary on Matthew 5.

great wonder of a wretched sinner being lifted out of the pit of sin and translated into the Kingdom of Light happen. Only in Christ!

Hebrews 2:14 (AMP) affirms the humanity of Jesus:

'Therefore, since [these His] children share in flesh and blood [the physical nature of mankind], He Himself in a similar manner also shared in the same [physical nature, but without sin], so that through [experiencing] death He might make powerless (ineffective, impotent) him who had the power of death—that is, the devil—'

JESUS, bearing the weight of our sins **(1 Peter 2:24)**, faced the full wrath of God, directed at Him only because our sins were laid upon Him **(Isaiah 53:5–6)**. In His final moments on the cross, He cried out, asking God why He had forsaken Him **(Matthew 27:46)**.

Anthropomorphism refers to the ascription of human qualities to God, who is Spirit, as a way of communicating higher truths about Him to us. For example, when God is described as sitting down **(Psalm 47:8)**, it is anthropomorphic. A related concept, anthropopathism, ascribes human emotions, such as joy or compassion, to God, helping us grasp the depth of His love in language we can understand.

Despite these figurative elements, we see the chief expression of God's love not in such metaphorical language but in Jesus. His joy, sadness, pain, and ultimately His sacrifice for us, are crystal-clear, tangible and fuller demonstrations of God's empathetic love and care for His people. When Jesus cried out in anguish on the cross, it was not a metaphor! He was abandoned by God, just like the scapegoat that bore the sins of the people at atonement (**Leviticus 16**). He carried the crushing weight of our sins to atone for us (**Isaiah 53:6**), while we received His righteousness. Despite the physical agony of the crucifixion, I do not believe that it could compare to the darkness of being forsaken by God. Jesus faced the reality of hell—total alienation from the goodness of God while being exposed to His wrath and judgement. And all for our sake; for you and for me.

You might easily accuse someone who tries to sympathise with your pain but hasn't experienced it themselves: '*You don't understand. You don't know what I am going through.*' But you cannot say that to someone who has lived through a similar experience.

I remember when I lost my brother, and the endless condolences poured in from those I held close enough to confide in. While I believed they genuinely loved me and grieved my pain, I also knew they could not *really* understand, by experience, the emptiness that threatened to swallow me or the sting in my heart each time it hit me that I would never see my brother again.

We cannot say to Jesus, '*You are God—high, mighty and untouchable—yet You are trying to save us from Your high heavens. You don't understand what it means to be human,*' because He *was* [and *is*] human. He was born of a virgin into a humble family, a carpenter's household. He was a helpless baby, needing the protection of the humans He came to save **(Matthew 2:13–14)**. He experienced hunger, fatigue and sleep. He felt grief **(John 11:35)**, faced disappointment, and endured hardships. He encountered shame, hatred and betrayal, not just from His creation, but from those closest to Him. As a man, He did not always know everything; He only knew what was revealed to Him by the Spirit of God. He, too, experienced the uncertainties of life.

In fact, Jesus, at the start of His ministry, was baptised as a symbol of identification with sinners, whom He came to save, even though He was sinless **(Matthew 3)**. His ministry was marked by close relationships with people society deemed outcasts **(Matthew 9:10–11)**.

Hebrews 1:1–2 (NIV):

1 In the past God spoke to our ancestors through the prophets at many times and in various ways,

2 but in these last days he has spoken to us by his Son, whom he appointed heir of all things, and through whom also he made the universe.

3 The Son is the radiance of God's glory and the exact representation of his being, sustaining all things by his powerful word. After he had provided purification for sins, he sat down at the right hand of the Majesty in heaven.

God came down from Heaven to become a man, His creation, just to save humanity. What a condescension! He died our death to give us life. I get goosebumps just thinking about it.

Imagine your pet dog fell ill with a strange sickness, and to save him, you would have to take the form of a dog, living as he does, teaching future generations how to overcome this sickness. You would not be able to speak, you would walk on all fours, and you would have to depend on your owner for food, water and care.

Then one day, all the other dogs would gather to falsely accuse you and subject you to the most humiliating treatment conceivable. Would you even consider doing that? But God did.

Jesus did not come merely to show us that He understands, by experience, what it means to be human. He came to teach us *how* to be human. As C.S. Lewis puts it in *Mere Christianity*:

> *'Did you ever think, when you were a child, what fun it would be if your toys could come to life? Well suppose you could really have brought them to life. Imagine turning a tin soldier into a real little man. It would involve turning the tin into flesh. And suppose the tin soldier did not like it. He is not interested in flesh: all he sees is that the tin is being spoilt. He thinks you are killing him. He will do everything he can to prevent you. He will not be made into a man if he can help it.*
>
> *The result of Christ's sacrifice is that you now had one man who really was what all men were intended to be: one man whom the created life, derived from His Mother, allowed itself to be completely and perfectly turned into the begotten life. He chose an earthly career which involved the killing of His human desires at every turn—poverty, misunderstanding*

from His own family, betrayal by one of His intimate friends, being jeered at and manhandled by the Police, and execution by torture. And then, after being thus killed—killed every day in a sense—the human creature in Him, because it was united to the divine Son, came to life again. The Man in Christ rose again: not only the God. That is the whole point. For the first time we saw a real man. One tin soldier—real tin, just like the rest—had come fully and splendidly alive.'

Athanasius puts it this way:

'Similarly, though He used the body as His instrument, He shared nothing of its defect, but rather sanctified it by His indwelling —'

THROUGH HIS LIFE, we see what God designed humanity to look like in its fullness: He was tempted in every way, as we often are, yet He never sinned **(Hebrews 4:15)**; He is the fulfilment of the Law **(Matthew 5:17; Ephesians 2:15)**, meaning that He perfectly kept the Law and every requirement it demanded.

We know that another effect of sin is that it restrains our emotions, making it difficult to express them without falling into sin. In Jesus, we see that it is possible to be fully human without giving into the flesh! Like Him, who perfectly expressed every emotion, we can be angry and not sin. We can express fear in ways that honour God; we can grieve without falling into sin.

Jesus mourned the cruel and tragic death of John the Baptist, beheaded by Herod, yet He still healed those who came to Him and then fed the five thousand immediately afterwards **(Matthew 14:13–21)**. I do not know that I would not abandon all my compassion and responsibilities if grief overtook me. *How about you?*

Jesus showed us that God created every one of our emotions with a purpose far beyond giving the devil a foothold in our lives.

He came to show us what to do to look like our Father once again. He came to repair our broken vision so that we can look at God directly rather than hide our faces as Adam did. He came to reveal the true image of the Father and how we were always meant to reflect Him.

Sometimes, we interpret God sending Jesus to mean that Jesus is kinder or more merciful than God. However, Jesus said in **John 6:44 (CSB), 'No one can come to me unless the Father who sent me draws him ...'** We cannot encounter or know Jesus unless God leads us to Him—the very Gospel we believe in reveals God's righteousness **(Romans 1:17)**. We cannot know God unless He first chooses to know us. There is access, and the option to say '*no,*' but only because He first opened the door. He made the first move.

The very name *Jesus* decreed before His birth through the Virgin Mary **(Matthew 1:21)** comes from the Latin form of the Greek *Yeshua*, which literally means 'Yahweh saves.' Yahweh, which means '*I am,*' is God's name.

And how could Jesus be kinder than God, when the Father and His Son are one **(John 10:30; 17:11)**? It helps to remember that many of the passages that shape our imagination of God as cruel and wicked come from Ancient Israel, before whom God was veiled. And even the Israelites always admitted that God was just for punishing their acts of wickedness—**Nehemiah 9:33 (NIV): 'In all**

that has happened to us, you have remained righteous; you have acted faithfully, while we acted wickedly.'

Yet through Jesus, we see God clearly, and God also sees us as justified through Christ. For us, the mystery has been revealed. In Jesus, we get to *really* know God! What a blessing.

13

SATAN, BE GONE

May I never see you as an angel of light.
May your offers never entice my senses.
—Maranatha

What is happening to our archenemy, Satan, as God rescues us from his bondage through Christ's ransom?

Recall that through the inroad of sin, Satan thrived in our lives. Because of our sinful nature and the debt we owed, he had the leeway to draw us deeper and deeper into the clutches of sin and farther away from God.

In fact, only the Israelites had a glimpse of God! The rest of the world, us Gentiles, were deep in the miry clay of sin and darkness.

Romans 6:21 (ESV) says, '**For when you were slaves of sin, you were free in regard to righteousness.**' Under the tyranny of the devil, Satan, we had no obligation to righteousness. We could not conceive of good, let alone do it.

However, when Jesus died and rose again, He rescued us from Satan's oppression. His atonement led to, as R.C. Sproul puts it, a *'cosmic victory over demonic principalities and powers.'* **Ephesians 1:21–22 (ESV)** explains that God **'seated him at his right hand in the heavenly places, far above all rule and authority and power and dominion, and above every name that is named, not only in this age but also in the one to come.'**

Athanasius makes it even clearer:

> *'When did people begin to abandon the worship of idols, unless it were since the very Word of God came among men? When have oracles ceased and become void of meaning, among the Greeks and everywhere, except since the Savior has revealed Himself on earth? When did those whom the poets call gods and heroes begin to be adjudged as mere mortals, except when the Lord took the spoils of death and preserved incorruptible the body He had taken, raising it from among the dead?'*

The ruler of this world, Satan, has been cast out. The time when he relentlessly oppressed us because we turned our backs on God is over **(John 12:31–32; 1 Peter 3:18–19; Zechariah 3; Revelation 12:7–11)**. Satan can no longer exploit our sin to bind us, for there is no longer any legal ground for such. Jesus paid the price in full!

What does this *really* mean? For one, we are no longer under any curses, whether generational or otherwise. Being born again [into the family of Christ] means that any former curses, whether from natural familial alliances or when we were sinners, no longer apply to us. Instead, Christ's blessings rest upon us.

I used to think of Satan as God's rival. But isn't it even logically inconsistent for a created being to be equal to its Creator? Satan, that old serpent, is certainly not God's mate. One command from the King would erase his existence. God has kept him on the scene for a reason.

Regardless, we must not think of Satan as completely impotent. He remains an accuser of the brethren—even though we are free from his accusations **(Revelation 12:10; Colossians 1:22)**. We are instructed to stay vigilant, for he prowls like a roaring lion, seeking whom to devour, fully aware that his time is short **(1 Peter 5:8; Revelation 12:12)**.

Satan continues to use deceit to lure us from God. A clear example is in **Acts 5**, where he **'filled their (Ananias and Sapphira) hearts to lie to the Holy Spirit.'** He is a liar, an enemy of the truth of God, who strives to tempt us and lead us astray **(Matthew 13:24–30; Luke 22:13)**.

His goal remains our rebellion against God. He pursues this end through various means: planting fear, doubt and other vices in our hearts; exploiting our besetting sins to entice us; interfering with the transmission of truth **(Matthew 13:38–39)**; and even sowing divisions within the church **(1 Timothy 4:1–2)**.

Satan desires to sift the believer like wheat **(Luke 22:31–32)**. We must take heed when life feels smooth, but the devil is having our faith for supper. Yet, Jesus prays for us, and God answers Him! He will not lose any of us **(1 Peter 1:5; Ephesians 1:19–20)**.

How do we resist him? By submitting to God **(James 4:7; Ephesians 6:10–20)**.

1 Peter 5:8–9 (CSB) gives us a very clear directive:

8 Be *sober-minded*, be alert. Your adversary the devil is prowling around like a roaring lion, looking for anyone he can devour.

9 Resist him, firm in the faith, knowing that the same kind of sufferings are being experienced by your fellow believers throughout the world.

We must be sober-minded. We must have sober discipline that allows us to think things through moment by moment, not just go through the motions of daily living.

We must meditate often and on the truth **(Philippians 4:8)**. We must. For if we don't, the world will fill our minds with lies, worries, and other things that do not please God but give the enemy a foothold in our lives.

Let us not be unaware of his devices. For how did Satan deceive Eve? In **Genesis 3**, he didn't approach Eve with forceful coercion. He simply dismissed the consequences of disobeying God and elevated the benefits of eating the forbidden fruit. He tempted her by twisting perspective.

We must remember that, no matter how seemingly small, walking with the enemy is walking against the good —God. God's instructions are not arbitrary; they are sacred boundaries that protect us, and stepping outside them carries weighty consequences. Every time we give in to sin, we numb our minds to God, dumb our intellect, and harden our hearts, like brute beasts **(Psalm 73:22)**.

Eve was deceived because her knowledge of the truth was subtly distorted. Keeping this in mind, let us seek the truth and constantly challenge the convictions we hold. In doing so, we will strengthen our faith.

Let us take heed: discernment and sobriety are our weapons, and obedience our shield; for the enemy always promises freedom while delivering bondage.

Let us not think ourselves *formidable* opponents of Satan, as if we have any strength of our own. Instead, let us run under the protection of our King, for the One who lives in us is greater than the one who rules the world! If we make it a habit to *consider* God, and all the ways He has loved us to the uttermost, if we are *'bold in this thought,'* we will *'defy the adversary, tread down his temptations, resist his schemings, renounce the world ... valiant for the truth.'* [1]

And in the end, when Jesus returns, Satan will forever be destroyed **(2 Thessalonians 2:8; Revelation 19:21)**.

Hallelujah!

1. Christ is All: *The Valley of Vision*, Arthur Bennett.

14

FOLLOW THE LEADER

Jesus does not only give us access to God, but a path to continually walk in.
—Maranatha

To look like God, we must look at Him. This is not a casual glance but a seeking gaze, one that pays attention because it desires something. In **Acts 3: 3–5 (NIV)**, Peter asked the lame beggar who pleaded for alms to 'Look!'

3 When he saw Peter and John about to enter, he asked them for money.
4 Peter looked straight at him, as did John. Then Peter said, "Look at us!"
5 So the man gave them his attention, expecting to get something from them.

This man looked with expectation, even though he expected something different from what he ended up receiving. Yet he looked. He paid attention. He rendered a *seeking gaze*. This is how we must look at God if we are to become like Him.

When we spend time around our family and friends, we naturally pick up some of their traits, mannerisms or habits. This happens because we have been spending time with them and observing them closely, so we begin to look like them [in mannerisms].

My little sister is the sibling who resembles me the most, not just in her facial structure but in her mannerisms as well. She won't admit it, but I'm certain I am her role model (she'll cringe and baulk at this, but thankfully, this is my book, not hers). An implication of this is that she has picked up a few of my habits and, sometimes, she even sounds like me. If my parents or other family members are not paying close attention, they often mistake my voice for hers and hers for mine.

And this is our aim: to behold God constantly so that when we show up, He shows up through us, using us according to His will. My sister can copy me because she sees in me traits that she finds valuable; do you look at God and see someone you want to be like?

Ephesians 5:1 (NLT):

Imitate God, therefore, in everything you do, because you are his dear children.

Our call as children is to look like our Father in every aspect of our lives.

Let's bring this down to earth so it is not something that sounds so out of reach. When someone annoys you, what is your natural tendency? Do you blurt out the first thing that comes to mind based on your irritation? Or can you pause, remembering that God is **'slow to anger' (Exodus 34:6)** and that self-control is a fruit of the Spirit, choosing instead to respond with patience rather than act impulsively?

In truth, we must aim to abide in God so fully that we do not always have to consciously *pause* before acting for our good and to His glory. Just as a branch that abides in the vine does not have to *pause* before bearing fruit—by abiding, it is fruitful—so too, out of the abundance within us, what is without flows forth **(Luke 6:45)**.

What is within you?

Following God in His ways and obeying His commands means walking with Him and understanding His character. In this way, no matter the circumstances we face, no matter how nuanced, we can act according to what we know to be true about Him. As per His incomprehensibility, we cannot know Him *fully*, yet we can know Him *truly*.

Joseph, when faced with an easy escape from his suffering through adultery, cried out: **'How can I do this great wickedness and sin against God?' (Genesis 39:9, ESV)**. This was a man who did not have the Law, yet he knew God in his heart, perhaps from his fathers, and followed Him diligently.

When I was younger, I loved Barbie cartoons so much. As the music played and the lyrics danced across the screen, I would try to copy them, but they disappeared too quickly. I had no authority over the remote control, so I devised an alternative plan: I found my older sister's music book, where she had written down all the lyrics, and I copied them into my own book. The next time I watched the cartoon, I would confidently sing along like I co-authored the song.

I cringe when I think about how obsessed I was with Barbie, but perhaps this sparks something in you. Have you ever loved something so much that you tried to make space for it in your life? Maybe it was adopting a British accent, so you watched every British movie you could find. Or perhaps it was looking like a particular celebrity, so you followed all their social media accounts and started dressing up and speaking like them.

This is how we treat idols. But why doesn't it occur to us to do the same with God? He is not just another idol. He is **THE** God of the universe. He is worthy of emulation, and this begins by paying rapt attention to His Word.

In my second year of walking with God, I fell deeply in love with **1 Corinthians 13:4–7 (CSB), 'Love is patient, love is kind. Love does not envy, is not boastful, is not arrogant, is not rude, is not self-seeking, is not irritable, and does not keep a record of wrongs. Love finds no joy in unrighteousness but rejoices in the truth. It bears all things, believes all things, hopes all things, endures all things.'**

I thought to myself, if these are all the qualities of love, and God is love, then these must be the qualities of God. I longed to embody them, imagining a life of peace and joy for myself and for those around me—*for loving God is loving our neighbours*—when I thought of a Maranatha who could be patient, kind, slow to anger, selfless, etc. I wanted that so dearly, for would I truly be a Christian if those closest to me could not see the *Christness* in me? So, I began to memorise **1 Corinthians 13:4–7**, repeating the verses every morning after my devotion, replacing the word 'love' with my name.

Many times, this daily recital led me to forgive people who had offended me the day before, and so it became a habit for me to let go of anger easily—this is the power of God's Word! It is not mere good advice, motivation or affirmation; it is the power of the Holy Ghost **(Ephesians 1:19)**! I would remember **'love is patient,'** and as the word sank into my consciousness, I would feel the ease as impatience literally left my body at the start of each day.

Haven't we seen the damage that anger, impatience, selfishness and every other vice not rooted in love can cause? Do we not see it every day in our world? What a difference it would make if each of us decided to imitate God as our Father and shine His light into every dark place. What peace would come if we immersed our souls in His Word!

I used to be that person who didn't think much about breaking my promises until I realised that one of God's defining traits is His faithfulness even despite the steady unfaithfulness of His people **(Exodus 34:6; Jeremiah 1:12)**. Understanding this, I made a commitment to always honour my word, not because I was so amazing at keeping promises, but because God had set an example for me and I chose to follow it, no matter the cost and no matter how insignificant—even for things like punctuality. It also taught me to guard my tongue: to be deliberate about making a promise, knowing I would have to keep it.

Do not be fooled: the Word of God is not merely letters on a page; it carries the active power of God. The Word is Jesus Christ **(John 1:1)**, so when we obey it, we are following the Leader—we are looking at God to look like Him. As I shared, the Word transformed my life not simply because I studied it. It transformed my life because I let it take root and applied it daily, by God's grace.

The little things shape the big things. Letting God's Word guide my life in small matters prepared me to seek His approval before making any big decisions.

When we come into Christ, we die to our old selves and put on **'the new self, created to be like God in true righteousness and holiness' (Ephesians 4:24, NIV)**. Our old selves struggled under sin, but our new selves, purchased by the blood of Jesus, have received dominion over sin, enabling us to pursue holiness through consecration.

Our new selves were created to reflect God! With our new selves, we can look at God to look like God; we can be patient, kind, and obey all Ten Commandments faithfully ... but not by our power.

Our Wonderful, Merciful Helper

Our rebellion gave the enemy an inroad into our lives. Adam's disobedience, his reliance on his wisdom, rather than God's command, granted the enemy access to our souls. It was like allowing an insider into a fortified camp —the destruction began from within.

It's no wonder Paul writes in **Romans 7:15 (NIV), 'I do not understand what I do. For what I want to do I do not do, but what I hate I do.'** This is the work of the flesh. And the flesh does not merely refer to our physical bodies, but to a way of thinking—an orientation of the heart and mind—that operates without God at its helm **(2 Chronicles 32:8).**

In **Genesis 3:7**, we see Adam and Eve sewing fig leaves together to cover themselves up after they'd sinned. This reveals one of sin's primary instincts: self-preservation rather than dependence on God. By heeding the serpent's words, Adam and Eve darkened their minds with a new system of thinking, one no longer anchored in God and His commands, but shaped by their own distorted wisdom. By eating from the Tree of the Knowledge of Good and Evil, they chose autonomy over obedience, and in doing so, gave the enemy an inroad to exploit. It is much like we're working against ourselves. We're under attack from the inside. We're the insiders helping the enemy against our own city!

However, God also had His inroad—by placing His Spirit within us, empowering us to obey Him. Since the real battle was internal, God did not again give laws written on stone tablets; instead, He wrote His Law on our hearts by the Holy Spirit once we believed! From ancient times, God had promised a day when He would pour out His Spirit on all flesh, renewing human hearts and inclining them towards His ways **(Jeremiah 31:33–34; Ezekiel 36:26–28; Joel 2:23; Acts 2:17, 32–33).**

Since sin rendered us spiritually dead, God gave us Jesus, so that we may receive new lives! For death is not merely the physical cessation of life but separation from God, who is life itself. As Jesus neared the end of His earthly ministry, He introduced us to the Holy Spirit, the One who helps us to follow the Master. The Holy Spirit is the third Person of the Trinity or Godhead, which also includes God the Father and the Son, Jesus Christ.

Speaking of His impending death and resurrection, Jesus said: **'It is for your benefit that I go away, because if I don't go away, the Counselor will not come to you. If I go, I will send him to you' (John 16:7, CSB).**

This Counsellor, the Holy Spirit, is the One who:

1. Guides us into all truth **(John 16:13).**
2. Reveals Jesus to us and forms His likeness in us, teaching us to live as He lived **(John 16:14).**
3. *Helps* us in our weaknesses and infirmities, interceding for us and strengthening us for the work that God has called us to do **(Romans 8:26).** *'If we ourselves feel that we are backsliding, let us turn to the Spirit of God, crying, "Give me life!" Let us direct the attention of our fellow Christians to the Spirit of God.'*[1]

While our inner being is awakened when we come into Jesus, we still need direction and help as we relearn what it means to be a child of God; for our sanctification is progressive **(Hebrews 10:14).** When a baby is born, they begin from scratch—learning how to walk, speak, and relate to the world around them. In the same way, when

1. Spurgeon's note on Micah 2:7.

we are born again, we start afresh, learning how to walk, speak, and live according to the ways of the Kingdom of God. This is where we need the *help* of the Holy Spirit, for we cannot imitate God by our strength.

The Holy Spirit is the source of our transformation; it is He who renews our minds as He works actively through the Word of God **(Romans 12:3)**. The Word itself carries the life-giving power of the Holy Spirit, which is why it is transformative in nature **(John 6:63)**. The Spirit does not work apart from the Word, neither is the Word alive apart from the Spirit—together, they renew, convict, instruct, and refine us from the inside out.

'For those who are led by the Spirit of God are the children of God' (Romans 8:14, NIV). The Holy Spirit is our seal of sonship and the proof that God abides in us **(Galatians 4:6; 1 John 3:24)**. As such, being led by the Holy Spirit is a defining mark of the Christian life.

Jesus always let the Spirit lead Him. He consistently did the will of God in complete obedience and trust. Since Jesus is the perfect model of our Christian faith, it follows that we, too, walk in His steps, surrendering our will to the Holy Spirit and allowing Him to guide every part of our lives.

> **Galatians 5:16** (AMP) says:
>
> **'But I say, walk habitually in the [Holy] Spirit [seek Him and be responsive to His guidance], and then you will certainly not carry out the desire of the sinful nature [which responds impulsively without regard for God and His precepts].'**

It is when we walk in the Spirit that we align with God and can follow Him faithfully. When we come into Jesus, we receive the Holy Spirit. The Bible affirms this: '**Wherefore I give you to understand, that no man speaking by the Spirit of God calleth Jesus accursed: and that no man can say that Jesus is the Lord, BUT by the Holy Ghost' (1 Corinthians 12:3, KJV)**. This is not a matter of feelings; we cannot even confess Jesus as Lord without the help of the Holy Spirit! Just as He was present at the beginning of creation **(Genesis 1:2)**, so He is present at the very beginning of our new life in Christ **(John 3:5–6)**. This is an unchanging truth.

The Holy Spirit enables us to know God *intimately*. Since only He knows the mind of God, He reveals the same to us so that we may walk in alignment with Him **(1 Corinthians 2:11)**.

He helps us to understand God's heart by taking from Jesus, who shares fully in the nature and mind of the Father.

John 16:14–15 (CSB):
14 He will glorify me, because he will take from what is mine and declare it to you.
15 Everything the Father has is mine. This is why I told you that he takes from what is mine and will declare it to you.

It is the Spirit's fruit that we are called to display in our daily lives **(Galatians 5:22–23)**. When we walk by the Holy Spirit, we will not gratify the desires of our flesh. But how do we walk by the Spirit? Simply by yielding to the

Word of God! For the Spirit never acts contrary to the Word; rather, His ministry is perfectly confirmed and empowered by it.

So far, we have encountered the triune God of the Bible: God the Father, who loves us, and predestines us for salvation through **God the Son,** Jesus, whom He sent to die for us. Our Saviour then sends **God the Holy Spirit** to us, the promised Helper, who is also the guarantee of our coming inheritance in Christ—eternal life **(Ephesians 1:4, 7, 13–14; John 14:16**).

The Holy Spirit continues the ministry of Jesus by helping us, teaching us, and bringing to our remembrance the truth of the Living Word. In doing so, He reveals Jesus to us more deeply, so that Christ may be glorified in our lives (**John 16:14–15**).

What next?

15

LOOKING AT GOD

A relationship is designed to be enjoyed; otherwise, it becomes a working arrangement.
—Maranatha

I never experienced true friendship until God committed my heart into the hands of this girl called Amanda (aka Damini, my damsel). Before Amanda, I had friends, but for some reason, we were never truly close because I never fully opened myself to anyone—I never let myself go. Friendships before her were often more transactional than genuine, because I held back and *loved* in a detached manner.

However, when Amanda came into my life, I realised that intimacy was not reserved for only husband and wife. I saw that all my previous friendships were just a sliver of the iceberg of true friendship. My earlier relationships were more transactional than unconditional; if I'd lost contact with any of those people, it would not have hurt much, and I would have moved on pretty easily. That is not what love looks like.

And certainly not with Amanda. I tell her from time to time that when we get old, I have to die first, because I would not know what to do without her in my life. She always thinks I am joking, but as David sang of Jonathan in **2 Samuel 1:26**, her love for me is more wondrous than the love of men (Amanda will disagree on this point, but again, this is my book, so ...).

I am writing this quasi-love letter to Amanda not just to make her smile, but to make you understand the difference between having a God in your life and having a relationship with God in your life.

Born into a Christian home, I had God in my life. I knew we worshipped Him, went to church every Sunday to sing to Him, and asked Him for favours now and then. But something significant was missing. It was not the head knowledge from Scripture—I had been well taught in Sunday School—but the relationship that was absent.

This was how I had friends before Amanda: we went to classes together, hung out, laughed and talked about boys. However, I never fully opened myself to them; I never truly trusted anyone with the things that weighed on my heart. There was no intimacy, little depth.

We cannot approach God with the same shallowness we use with people. Too often, we want to walk *safely* with God. We're afraid of getting heartbroken, so we keep our secrets and hopes to ourselves to avoid disappointment. We hesitate to give God our hearts fully, to surrender our wills completely, because human beings around us have hurt us when we let our walls down. We think:

What if He fails me?

What if He does not come through?

What if He disappoints me?

What if everyone but me has a testimony?

What if my prayers are not answered?

These fears are valid, but so is this truth: with God, it cannot be anything but deep. It is all the way or no way for Yahweh. **'He wants us—all or nothing' (1 Corinthians 10:22, MSG).**

In an earlier chapter, we explored how a person can know God in one way but not in another, even though He is all things. If, for example, you have experienced God the Provider but not God the Healer, this does not make Him any less a healer; it simply means you have not yet experienced that facet of His being. Many Christians know God as a glorious and awe-inspiring Creator, but have not received a revelation of Him as their Father. The effect of this is very obvious in their lives.

First, they may fear God but hesitate to draw close to Him, perhaps because of a traumatic experience with their father or a father figure.

Second, they obey Him, but only out of an ungodly fear of punishment.

Third, they mistrust His intentions for them.

Fourth, they struggle to believe in His Word.

Fifth, they keep expecting God to turn against them or go back on His promises.

Sixth, even when God remains faithful, providing visible evidence time and again, they just have a difficulty seeing God as a responsible Father who has never—and will never—let them down.

Seventh, they know that God is good, but they do not expect Him to be good to them.

Eighth, they feel they must earn God's affection and have a hard time returning to God after they fail or stumble.

These are only a handful of consequences, as the effects can take a variety of forms. And it is understandable: fatherhood is a sacred responsibility and many fathers—as a result of sin—have fallen short, thus distorting the beautiful picture of fatherhood as God intended it.

However, God is your first Father **(Ephesians 3:15; 4:6)**. He is the Father of fathers **(1 Corinthians 8:6)**, and even if others fail to live up to an exemplary standard, He does not, for He Himself is the standard of fatherhood.

I am fortunate to have been raised in a family where I saw my father live up to a considerable degree to God's idea of fatherhood. He has always been there for my siblings and me, sacrificing everything he could to give us the best. Yet, as I grow, I also see and understand his failings because he is only human. A human being cannot be the standard; only God can. We must stop allowing fallen humans to turn us away from the fullness of goodness found in a relationship with our Father.

This is where faith comes in. **Hebrews 11:6 (AMP)** says: **'But without faith it is impossible to [walk with God and] please Him, for whoever comes [near] to God must [necessarily] believe that God exists and that He rewards those who [earnestly and diligently] seek Him.'**

This faith is not merely a tool for supplication; it is the very means by which we experience God, seeking His will to be done because we know it will be for His glory and for our utmost good. We become Christians in the first place by believing in the finished work of Christ, but it doesn't end there. We continue to walk with Him by the same faith and not by sight **(2 Corinthians 5:7)**, which means we must live by and elevate God's Word—which delineates His character—far above what our physical eyes perceive and above the alternate narratives we have been fed about love and fatherhood. For carnal sight breeds ungodly fear.

Your faith must draw you closer, you see. For when you take a step close to God, He takes an innumerable amount towards you **(James 4:8)**. Faith is trusting God, even—perhaps especially—when it seems illogical. Regardless, our Christian faith is not baseless or contrary to evidence. Our trust is in the One for whom impossible is nothing; who sacrificed in love for us, even before we knew we owed a debt **(Romans 5:8)**. He has taken the first step already—shouldn't you take yours?

Your Father calls you. He desires a relationship with you, His child. He will never relent in taking responsibility for every area of your life if only you let Him in. God is not agnostic about anything. He cares for you. At your every joy, He beams; at your every sorrow, His heart breaks. His arms remain open to you.

The Israelites had generational experience of staggering at the promises of God. They were a faithless bunch (as we often can be), and they grumbled tirelessly. Their grumbling was sinful because it belittled God's power and Word. It undermined the very promises He had given them and His power to fulfil them! And yet, He always returned to discipline and save them, over and again. What a Father!

Faith is a central ingredient of our personal walk with God. It is by faith that we please Him. When spiritual eyes are opened, they often contradict what is seen in the physical realm; only with faith can we stand firm.

Take Elisha's fearful servant in **2 Kings 6:16–17**, for example. He and his master, Elisha, were surrounded by enemy soldiers, and, rightfully, he was afraid. However, when Elisha prayed, and God opened this servant's eyes to see the heavenly chariots of fire protecting them, we see that his fear only existed because he could not *see* [through the eyes of faith].

As physical realities contradict and belittle our spiritual reality, we are urged to *fight the good fight of faith* (**1 Timothy 6:12, KJV**). Faith becomes a fight as we contend in this physical world.

But how do we have faith? It is not something we can manufacture with our minds. Faith is a tangible gift from God that enables us to look at Him, and it is strengthened the more we maintain that gaze! **'Looking to Jesus, the founder and perfecter of our faith, who for the joy that was set before him endured the cross, despising the shame, and is seated at the right hand of the throne of God' (Hebrews 12:2, ESV)**. We have a model who endured the cross. When we fix our eyes on Him, the joy set before us, we too can endure the sufferings of this world.

It is for this reason that Paul prayed, **'that the eyes of your heart [the very center and core of your being] may**

be enlightened [flooded with light by the Holy Spirit], so that you will know and cherish the hope [the divine guarantee, the confident expectation] to which He has called you, the riches of His glorious inheritance in the saints (God's people), and [so that you will begin to know] what the immeasurable and unlimited and surpassing greatness of His [active, spiritual] power is in us who believe. These are in accordance with the working of His mighty strength' (Ephesians 1:18–19, AMP).

This is what faith unlocks! It helps us grasp more deeply what God has called us to and the hope that we have, so that we do not undermine the all-encompassing gift of salvation or compare ourselves with the world.

When I first gave my life to Christ, I lost a romantic relationship. I can never forget that day. I went to Amanda's house, and my tears flowed freely. I considered my imminent loneliness and all the effort and resources I had invested to make it work. It hurt terribly.

But then, I considered my gains: eternal life and, above all, an unexplainable peace. Even while my eyes bled, there was such a rest in my soul that I knew I'd made the right decision.

The world is shiny and tempting, but it is that thing which glitters and is not gold. We must be armed with faith to see as God does, so we do not despise the gift of salvation and self-sabotage because we cannot perceive certain realities in the physical. We are called to live by faith!

There should be no problem this world presents to us that we cannot face by remembering, *'Jesus died for me,'* and holding to heart all that this means. As Spurgeon beautifully notes,

> *'There is not a promise, not a word in the Bible that is not ours. In the depths of tribulation, it will comfort. In the midst of waves of distress, it will cheer. When sorrows surround, it will be our helper.'*

To represent God well, to see as He does through the eyes of faith, we must look at Him. Think of a prince being groomed to inherit his father's throne; you would hardly expect him to go gallivanting around town. In the same way, why not start acting like the heir of God that you are? You are made in the image of the one true and living God! You look like Him! It is a privilege, but you are mistaken if you do not realise that it is also a responsibility.

It is Christ who allows us to look at God and truly see Him. God blessed us with breath, rain, and many other common graces, as inhabitants of the earth, so that we might, perhaps, marvel at the beauty of our existence and seek out our Creator **(Acts 17:25–27; Romans 1:20).**

But we did not. Instead, we turned away and idolised created things. Some have even looked at the glory of the skies and declared that there is no God; these very skies that proclaim God's glory **(Psalm 19)**. What folly.

In Christ, we can look at God. Through His sacrificial blood that cleanses us from sin, we can enter into God's holy presence to behold Him and glorify Him. Hitherto, we were lost in darkness and could not commune with God. His holiness was a fearful thing to us while we were sinners. But now, we can *really* see Him. His holiness, which we could formerly not comprehend, we now seek to imitate **(1 Peter 1:15–16)**.

But what does looking at God actually entail? Let us begin with a closer examination of the anchor text, **2 Corinthians 3:18.**

The New Covenant

> **We all, with UNVEILED FACED, are LOOKING as in a MIRROR at the GLORY OF THE LORD and are being TRANSFORMED into the same image FROM GLORY TO GLORY; this is FROM THE LORD who is the Spirit (2 Corinthians 3:18; CSB).**

This popular text comes from Paul's second letter to the Corinthians. In this chapter, he draws a comparison between the Old and New Covenants. He argues, in summary, that the New Covenant is not like the Old Covenant but is far more glorious. This is highlighted in several key differences:

The Old Covenant was written on tablets of stone, while the New Covenant is written on our hearts (verse 3).

The Old Covenant is the letter of the Law, which kills **(Romans 7:5–6)**, while the New Covenant is of the Spirit, who gives life (verse 6).

The Old Covenant brings condemnation while the New Covenant brings righteousness (verse 9).

The Old Covenant had a fading glory, while the New

Covenant has a surpassing and enduring glory (verses 10–11).

> Giving a commentary on this, Guzik quotes Poole,
>
> *'And although the gospel came not into the world as the law, with thunder, lightning, and earthquakes; yet that was ushered in by angels, foretelling the birth and office of John the Baptist, and of Christ; by the great sign of the virgin's conceiving and bringing forth a Son; by a voice from Heaven, proclaiming Christ the Father's only begotten Son, in whom he was well pleased.'*

The Old Covenant was received with fear and through a veil **(Hebrews 12:18–19).** God was not seen by the people with whom He covenanted. God Himself told Moses, **'Go down and warn the people not to break through to SEE the Lord; otherwise many of them will die' (Exodus 19:21, CSB).**

The New Covenant, by contrast, was received with love and through clear sight. For Jesus, who is God, sat in plain sight with His disciples and declared the New Covenant through the breaking of bread (His body) and drinking of wine (the pouring out of His blood) at the Last Supper **(Luke 22:19–20).**

As He died, the temple's curtain was torn in two, symbolising a hitherto absent access.

Our ingress to the presence of God, our desire and ability to look at God, is a central aspect of this New Covenant!

We come with *unveiled faces*. Moses wore a veil when he addressed the people with the Law, but in the presence of God, he removed it. We do not look at God through our masks or inflated self-egos. We must come as we are into the freedom of God's presence.

We *look*. This is not a glance or a fleeting glimpse. The idea of *beholding* connotes a careful, sustained attention—a studying gaze. We must come seeking. We must come with a desire to know God as an end in itself.

As in a *mirror*. The mirrors of ancient times were not like the mirrors we have today—they were made from polished glass or metals (like bronze) and, as such, didn't reflect with clarity or precision. It was these blurred mirrors Paul had in mind as he wrote to the Corinthians. What we see now is not perfectly clear, because what we possess is imperfect. The fullness of our salvation, being able to see God as He is, cannot be realised in the mortality we currently don. For now, we know Him truly, but not fully. It is when Jesus comes that we shall see clearly [and have, become] what is perfect **(1 John 3:2–3)**.

We behold *the glory of God*. We do not come to see ourselves; we come to see God. We behold His holiness, His perfection, His majesty and splendour, and attempt imitation.

We are *transformed*. Our hearts change, so our lives change. We do not remain as we were when we first came.

From *glory to glory*. Our transformation is continuous until that perfect day when Jesus returns to complete us, where nothing can be added or taken away. Our metamorphosis is not an undulating one where we return often to our sins and then leap to the cross to start over. Rather, it is a constant leap from God to God.

This entire process is *from the Lord*. It is not by works.

Since we could not even look because we wished to, but because Christ prompted us to, let us not think that it is our beholding that contains our salvation.

> *'Our sufficiency is of God; let us practically enjoy this truth. We are poor, leaking vessels, and the only way for us to keep full is to put our pitcher under the perpetual flow of boundless grace.'* —Spurgeon.

Our enduring transformation is one that will be perfected, but only by beholding the true God, not a false one. The true God is revealed in Scripture; let us comply with this revelation. For if we behold a false god, we will also be transformed into the same image **(Psalm 115:8).**

How, then, do we discern with whom we commune? If we claim to commune with Christ, but do not display the same fruits of His character as revealed in Scripture and to the end of eternal salvation, we may, in fact, be fellowshipping with a false Christ.

God's presence is a gift to us; it is an access that was hitherto absent, especially for us Gentiles. We must feel the Psalmist's laments in **Psalm 51**, where he pleads that God should not take him away from His presence. God's presence is our very life.

Jesus, on the cross and for sin, was cast away from God's presence so that we might be ushered in. His sacrifice was to ensure that we would not face crushing, eternal alienation from God's presence, as in hell. For even on earth, every human still enjoys the reality of God's presence and common graces, whether or not they follow Him.

God's presence is also freedom for us **(v17)**. Let us not think this freedom to be bondage and look lustingly at the world that is *freely* heading towards its doom. God has saved us from: the bondage of sin, so we have freedom in life; the penalty of sin (eternal death), so we have freedom in death; the guilt of sin; the dominion of sin and fear of the Law; and the fear of death and hell.

Consequently, we are saved to all of God's promises in His Word and may now approach the throne of grace with confidence, having received a right to Heaven.

What glory! Ours is the radiance described in **Psalm 34:5 (CSB)**, **'Those who look to him are radiant with joy; their faces will never be ashamed.'**

Our Responsibility

What does *looking at God* look like in our daily lives?

In **Numbers 21**, the people of Israel sinned against God by their unbelief, which led to murmuring. In judgement, God sent poisonous snakes among them, whose bites caused the deaths of many. When the people cried out for mercy, Moses interceded on their behalf. God instructed him to make a bronze snake and mount it on a pole, declaring that whoever looked at it would be healed.

Now, this makes no logical sense—looking at a representation of the very cause of their sin upon a stick to receive healing—but it worked, solely because the Lord commanded it. This is the place of faith! For, in time, this same bronze snake became an object of idolatry among the Israelites and had to be destroyed **(2 Kings 18:4).**

Through Jesus, we come to understand that the bronze snake foreshadowed His death on a cross for the salvation of humanity.

As John 3:14–16 (CSB) declares:
14 Just as Moses lifted up the snake in the wilderness, so the Son of Man must be lifted up,
15 so that everyone who believes in him may have eternal life.
16 For God loved the world in this way: He gave his one and only Son, so that everyone who believes in him will not perish but have eternal life.

And this is the first aspect of looking at God: it is beholding the cross of Jesus in faith, so that we may be healed, and continually healed, of our wickedness. It is grasping the depth of His sacrifice for you, the great price He paid, and reflecting that same love to the people around you. For we love because He first loved us.

Looking at God means carrying our crosses. Christ clearly said that the one who would follow Him must deny themselves and take up their cross daily **(Luke 9:23).** We cannot know *self* and know God. We cannot cling to our own dreams and ambitions and mask them with a veneer of devotion. To behold God is to surrender our entire being to Him, saying, *'Do with me as You will.'* But we must truly mean such a request, for these are the kinds of petitions our King delights in, and He does not fail to act quickly in the matter. If we cannot give up everything we hold dear, we cannot follow Jesus **(Luke 14:33)**. Praise be to Him, for we have much more to gain! If the thought of *losing* anything for God saddens us, like that rich young ruler, then we have unduly embraced the world, and we must let go.

Looking at God means actively seeking Him, and His kingdom, for He is worthy to be found. And what is the kingdom of God? It is righteousness, peace and joy in the Holy Ghost expressed through the fruit of the Holy Spirit **(Galatians 5:22–23)** that reveal we are at peace with God and He is at peace with us. This is what uplifts the soul.

Through consistent devotion, we must cast ourselves daily at His feet, in the Word and in prayer. We cannot afford to behold anything else, whether man or matter, before we have looked to God; it is by seeking Him first that our discernment is sharpened and we receive the strength to handle whatever life throws our way each day.

Furthermore, the discipline of devotion requires two important things:

That our minds are rationally engaged. Whether we read our Bibles or pray, it cannot be a mindless activity—our minds cannot be absent. For God calls us to love Him with our minds. Therefore, devotion is an act of rational worship. It must be intelligible, and meaning communicated that blesses our minds and intellects. We must pray, especially in our understanding. For it is in devotion that we know more about God—His character, will and ways, which in turn helps us know ourselves better—as well as our [besetting] sins, longings, weaknesses, and endless dependence on grace.

For this reason, meditation is also an essential part of our communion with God. It is the *holy pause* between hearing and speaking—the deliberate pondering upon God's truth until it seeps into our affections and reshapes our desires. Without meditation, Scripture becomes information and prayer, mere speech. With meditation, our hearts are renewed, and our life continuously conforms to Christ's.

Second, that we remain until we are truly restored. Our prayers to God are not an act of philanthropy, like He needs them, but an exchange **(Philippians 4:6–7; Matthew 11:28–30)**. We come with our petitions and thanksgiving, and He gives us His peace and rest. We may not depart until our hearts are genuinely at rest. It is not measured by the minutes we spend, but by the peace we receive—whether it takes five minutes or three hours. As our appetites are transformed, we recognise that only God can truly satisfy us. We must allow Him to satisfy us each day, giving us our daily bread.

And praise be to God, for when we approach Him in prayer, repentance and worship, the least we receive is His very self! Let us not make the mistake of treating God like a genie when He is the true reward. He is our reward! Let us not despise this extraordinary gift!

The Israelites of old needed a priest to access God. They could offer nothing to Him nor hear from Him without the high priest. Imagine needing to hear from God and having to go to the church (this is a gross understatement, considering modern technology). In fact, you would have to take a day off just to worship in the temple. But today, we can sit in our rooms and speak to God directly, for our High Priest, the God-Man, intercedes unceasingly for us. If an Israelite of those times were to hear of this access we now enjoy, they would think it incredible, and perhaps feel a touch envious. *Ah*. May we truly understand what we have!

Looking at God means taking a genuine interest in the faith we profess. It means being diligent students of God's Word, studying to show ourselves approved so we do not distort the truth when we speak or in how we live **(2 Timothy 2:15).**

We also look at God through obedience. For when we obey, what we are really saying is, *'My King, I do not hold on to my ways. I trust Your love for me not only in this world but in the one to come.'* And we must not be ashamed of the results of our obedience. God is concerned not with the outcome but with our transformation. Each time we obey Him, we look more like Him. He is the true outcome of our obedience. Our greatest gift!

Looking at God is living a life worthy of our calling in Christ. Our call is to be holy as He is. It is rejoicing in God, finding our joy always in Him. It is living a quiet life, marked by gentleness and meekness, fretting less and trusting God more.

Looking at God means loving Him with exertion. For if our call is to love God with all our heart and mind and strength, then we must desire God with, and in, our inner and outer parts.

Think of that game, Tug of War, where two sides hold on to a rope and have to pull the other side over a central line to win. It is an exerting, exhausting game. All the times I've played it, I had to mentally prepare myself never to let go of the rope, for a momentary lapse could mean loss. It is a game of stretched will and taut muscles. Such is the exertion we must employ to love God.

When it is easier to laugh at a crass joke, we must strengthen our hearts and consider our King's holiness. When it is easier to listen to sounds that do not glorify Him, we must reach forward and press stop. When sinful thoughts arise, unseen by outside eyes, we must put away such bruteness and honour God with pleasing thoughts. When it is easier to stay in bed, we must rouse ourselves and awaken every fibre of our being to worship Him. When it is easier to sit in the company of fools who dishonour Christ with their lips, we must either stand and proclaim Him or walk away—as the situation calls for. We must love Him with our entirety. And loving God means hating sin, not out of fear or for the sake of consequences, but because we love Him with all our hearts.

And let us help our souls by surrounding ourselves with the things that lift our gaze heavenward. It is folly to go to a nightclub to praise God; go to a church instead. It is self-deceit to follow worldly social media accounts, consume their content, then lament when your heart no longer longs for God. It is fraudulent to keep the wrong company and then cry out about the poor counsel you receive—can a bad tree produce good fruit? You cannot feast on the world and expect to reflect God. Let us take responsibility for our own spiritual health.

Looking at God means seeking the good of others, for Christianity is an other-centred faith (**1 Corinthians 10:24; Philippians 2:3–5, 21, 27; Genesis 18; Matthew 16:23**). We are called not merely to love ourselves but to love God and our fellow humans. The beauty and challenge of this command is that, in practice, these loves are inseparably linked. God loves people deeply; if we truly love Him, we will also love our neighbours.

This love looks like lifting your family (biological and spiritual) and your friends in prayer, presenting their desires before God as you thank Him for their lives. It looks like sending words of encouragement and exhortations to them often. It looks like paying attention to them, thinking of their needs, and seeking ways to serve them. Loving our neighbours means engaging with their spiritual journeys: checking if they are running the race to Heaven—and if they have strayed, praying for them and gently drawing them back.

It looks like laying down your life for them and sacrificing your comfort for their good. It looks like constant forgiveness, even when no apology is offered. It looks like generosity, providing material help when you can. Above all, it looks like caring, *really* caring and showing that you do. True love does not keep a safe distance to avoid hurt; it embraces pain as long as it leads to the good of the other.

A Scripture I hold close to my heart is that one where the righteous Judge separates the sheep from the goats in **Matthew 25.** The sheep were those who had cared for the hungry, the thirsty, the sick, and the needy. God declared that whatever they had done for these lowly ones, they had done for Him. Isn't that remarkable? The next time you are tempted to withhold good from another to whom it is due when it is in the power of your hands to do it, ask yourself, *'Am I withholding good from God?'*

And we must not wait for such opportunities to find

us; we should actively seek them out. As David sat in his palace, pondering on what to do for God **(2 Samuel 7)**, let us also ponder how we can love God and His people more deeply. In doing so, God may bless these desires and strengthen us to carry them out faithfully.

We will find that when we practise such things as are listed here, our gazes are naturally lifted to Heaven. It is not an easy task, for even in our physical composition, what feels most comfortable is a forward gaze, not an upward one—perhaps Adam had such a gaze in Eden when He fellowshiped with God. Here lies a warning, then, that perhaps, the greatest danger of our fallen nature may not be when we find ourselves looking downward at the material, for then we would clearly be in need of rescue. Rather, it is when we idolise convenience and comfort—a certain lukewarmness—in what we think we already know that we have no desire to press forward into better things.

But we must press on. So, let us press on!

PHILIPPIANS 3: 10–12 (NIV):

I want to know Christ—yes, to know the power of his resurrection and participation in his sufferings, becoming like him in his death, and so, somehow, attaining to the resurrection from the dead. Not that I have already obtained all this, or have already arrived at my goal, but I press on to take hold of that for which Christ Jesus took hold of me.

. . .

THIS IS OUR CHARGE: to know Christ and take hold of that for which He took hold of us—life in Him now and the fullness of eternal life to come **(1 Corinthians 9:24; 1 Timothy 6:12; Colossians 3:1–4)**. Every sacrifice we make to conform to Christ will be worth it when, on that day, we hear: '*Well done, good and faithful servant, enter into the joy of your Master.*'

The good news is that God is also looking at us! He is not absent-minded but intentional. He promises, **'I will instruct you and teach you in the way you should go; I will counsel you [who are willing to learn] with My eye upon you' (Psalm 32:8, AMP).** This is proof of His presence, mindfulness, and intimacy with us. He is El-Roi, the God who sees us **(Genesis 16:13)**. And He is not an aloof master; He also desires friendship with us **(James 2:23)**.

Numbers 6:26 (KJV) says, '**The Lord lift up his countenance upon thee, and give thee peace.**' This countenance [face] of the Lord is often translated as *favour* in other Bible versions. This echoes **Psalm 44:3 (KJV)**, where David describes God's countenance as His favour, which gave His people victory. What a comfort, what a joy!

When we look at Him, even as He looks at us, our sight is reshaped by His. We begin to see as He does.

Seeing like God entails believing in the integrity of the Word. When God says something, it is as good as done, for He watches over His Word to perform it **(Isaiah 55:11)**. Trust Him.

Seeing like God means discerning the distinction between what is good and what is truly godly. The Christian's distinction is not between good and bad; we're done having any conversation with sin. Our daily choice is between what seems good and what is *really* godly; those grey areas where our loyalty to our King is tested. We must choose what is godly over what merely seems 'right' to do, and pursue what God actually wants us to do (**1 Corinthians 6:12**). For this, we pray for wisdom for discernment. Seek Him.

Seeing like God means living set-apart lives so that we glorify Him among those who do not know Him **(Daniel 3:24–30; 6:26)**. Show Him.

Seeing as God means living with eternity in view—detached from the fleeting values of this world, expectant of Jesus' Second Coming, and actively partnering with Him to see His will to be done on earth as it is in Heaven **(Matthew 9:37–38; Jude 1:23)**. It means being a solution for the world, not conforming to it. Set your eyes on Him.

Seeing like God is being dependent on the Word, following Jesus' example. In the wilderness, He resisted every temptation with Scripture, not strength. Meditate on Him.

Seeing through God's eyes means practising His presence—being conscious of God's omni-qualities and then acting accordingly. It is knowing that we are God's temples, that He dwells in us, and living a life that honours this reality. It is telling the cab driver to turn off the carnal music blaring through the speakers because it does not please the Holy Spirit within us, so we cannot entertain it. Live for Him.

Seeing like God is understanding that suffering doesn't signify God's absence. Paul had a thorn in his flesh, and he spent long periods in prison, yet even these trials became a testimony of God's grace! Abase and abound in Him.

Seeing like God means living a life of service. As Jesus said, **'For even the Son of Man did not come to be served, but to serve, and to give his life as a ransom for many' (Mark 10:45, CSB).** Deny yourself for Him.

Seeing like God means refusing to entertain evil—not only because the consequences of sin extend beyond what we can see, but also because we are loyal to Him and recognise that every sin is ultimately against Him. When we sin, God is absent to us at that moment. Therefore, we must practice His presence consciously.

> *'Omnipresence yields good cheer to those who are panting for God.'*—Spurgeon

The end of our salvation is our glorification with Christ: only in this perfect state will we see God as He is. And this is our ultimate desire, to see God, even if we are not always conscious of it. For nothing but God can truly satisfy us **(Revelation 21–22).**

Choose in your heart today to give your all to your Father, who has already taken the first step toward you. God has come down to meet you; now you must rise to meet Him. Keep in the Narrow Way of salvation and walk in it, living wholly by His Word. In doing so, you will reflect the perfection of your Father in Heaven. This is life and peace for you.

And here we must again beware: there is a sense in which we can become falsely religious, performing our devotion to God only out of duty rather than delight. There is a way to *Christian* that drains all the joy and happiness from following and knowing God—when the *doing* becomes so tedious that we forget the *becoming*—that ultimate end, which is God. In such testing seasons, it helps to remember our purpose: the reason for which we were made.

The Westminster Catechism puts it in such a crisp, memorable way that I find no need for reduction. The question is: '*What is the chief end of man?*' The answer is: '*To glorify God, and to enjoy Him forever.*'

Our looking at God to look like Him may indeed be a labour, yes, and God is worth our toil, but it is not without blessings and rewards that redeem our weary souls—this is our enjoyment! There is not only a coming perfection to anticipate; there are also many joys that God gives to His children even while we remain on earth, chief of which is Himself. If we place God's glorification at the centre of everything, if we constantly meditate on His faithfulness, we will find joy in everything from work to play.

We were not made to wear ourselves out with toil, eating the bread of sorrow, anxious about the coming days. Instead, God invites us to lay down our burdens at His feet and take up His light yoke **(Matthew 11:28–30; Psalm 127:2)**. And this is not a one-time exchange; we must daily be devoted, because the world is quite inventive in the ways it places new, ungodly burdens on our shoulders to wear our hearts out and question whether following Christ is truly worth it.

The solution remains the same—look. God is never far from the man who asks for His help.

I find it fitting to end this chapter with a quote from C.S. Lewis' *Mere Christianity*:

'If we let Him ... He will make the feeblest and filthiest of us into a god or goddess, a dazzling, radiant, immortal creature, pulsating all through with such energy and joy and wisdom and love as we cannot now imagine, a bright stainless mirror which reflects back to God perfectly (though, of course, on a smaller scale) His own boundless power and delight and goodness. The process will be long and in parts very painful; but that is what we are in for. Nothing less.'

16

NEW VISION: REFLECTING CHRIST

The cross was a public display, so should our faith be.
—Maranatha

Sometimes, I let my mind wander, imagining where we might be if our first parents had not eaten the forbidden fruit.

What would the Garden of Eden look like now?

Would God have planted more gardens to accommodate a growing human population?

Would some descendants of Adam eventually have yielded to temptation, creating a divide—some remaining in the Garden, while the sinners would be forced to leave?

Looking back can be heavy with sadness and regret over what could have been, especially when it feels like the choice was taken right out of our hands. Yet, the future remains bright, overflowing with so much promise in Jesus.

What happens when we accept Christ?

What should be our next course of action?

Here is a question clue: from the beginning, what did God have in mind when He created humans? Yes, dominion, but at the core of it was this, **'Let us make human beings in our image, TO BE LIKE US. They will reign over the fish in the sea, the birds in the sky, the livestock, all the wild animals on the earth, and the small animals that scurry along the ground' (Genesis 1:26, NLT).**

God created you and me to be like Him! The first Adam failed in that calling, but in the second Adam, Jesus, we resume the ministry we were always meant to fulfil: to be *like* God **(Romans 5:12, 14)**. Everything God has revealed is aimed at restoring His image in us. The Law, the commandments, the parting of the Red Sea, the fall of Jericho ... all of it points to one purpose: that we might look at Him to look like Him.

These mighty acts are not miracles to God; they are miracles to us. To Him, they are simply expressions of who He is. God is not performing feats to impress us or prove His power to us—He has nothing to prove. What He desires is our love. Our trust. He wants us.

God, our good Father, shapes our character, building resilience in us that we may look more and more like Him —loving unconditionally, steadfast in the face of hardships, giving our all for Him, stewarding well what He has entrusted to us and travelling *light* in anticipation of eternity with Him. He is forming in us citizens of Heaven! He is forging Himself in us. Far beyond material dreams and goals, looking at God is fixing our gaze on eternity. Everything else—miracles, material experiences and enjoyment—is just a reminder for us to lift our gaze, again and again, in the realisation that *'there is more where this came from. There's God.'* For from Him, through Him and to Him are all things!

It is deeply ironic that God created Adam to be like Himself, yet the serpent tempted Eve with the very thing God had already given them. The serpent said, **'For God doth know that in the day ye eat thereof, then your eyes shall be opened, and ye shall be AS Gods, knowing good and evil' (Genesis 3:5, KJV).**

This remains the pattern of the enemy; he offers us something that *appears* better than what we already possess simply by being in God! To Adam and Eve, he offered the illusion of independence—being gods unto themselves rather than living under God's loving authority. He tempted them with self-rule instead of service. God Himself confirms in **Genesis 3:22** that the humans He created had indeed become 'like gods,' indeed, knowing good and evil. They no longer wanted God to define what was right and wrong for them; the same posture which has echoed through the ages to this very day. We see it in that era described in **Judges 21:25**, where everyone did what seemed right in their own eyes.

How well has that gone for us? A cursory glance around us answers.

In the temptation of Jesus, the devil offered Him everything that was already His, but through a shortcut that avoided the cross and, by extension, our salvation

(Matthew 4:8–9). Why, then, did Satan still make the offer? Because we sometimes fail to live in the awareness and reality of what already belongs to us. Adam and Eve were unwilling to pay the price of submission to God's authority and wisdom. Jesus was.

Thank God for the Holy Spirit, our Helper, through whom Jesus overcame the temptation. **'What we have received is not the spirit of the world, but the Spirit who is from God, so that we may UNDERSTAND what God has freely given us' (1 Corinthians 2:12, NIV).** As the Holy Spirit helps us grasp this incomprehensible gift we have in Christ, we become far less likely to accept Satan's trivial offers to turn away from God. For how shall we escape if we neglect so great a salvation? **(Hebrews 2:1–4).** We must give careful attention to God's Word, for it is what preserves us.

Our purpose in Christ, then, is summed up beautifully in **2 Corinthians 5:15 (NIV), 'And he died for all, that those who live should no longer live for themselves but for him who died for them and was raised again.'**

Our goal in Christ is to live for Him. We have given Him our ~~life~~ death, and collected His life in salvation, so our lives are not ours but His. **Romans 8:28–29 (NIV)** reminds us, **'And we know that in all things God works for the good of those who love him, who have been called according to his purpose. For those God foreknew he also predestined to be CONFORMED to the image of his Son, that he might be the firstborn among many brothers and sisters.'**

Here is a lengthy quote that almost thoroughly

describes what our new life in Christ should look like. Please pay close attention as you read.

Ephesians 4:17–32 (NIV):

'So I tell you this, and insist on it in the Lord, that you must no longer live as the Gentiles do, in the futility of their thinking. They are darkened in their understanding and separated from the life of God because of the ignorance that is in them due to the hardening of their hearts. Having lost all sensitivity, they have given themselves over to sensuality so as to indulge in every kind of impurity, and they are full of greed.

That, however, is not the way of life you learned when you heard about Christ and were taught in him in accordance with the truth that is in Jesus. You were taught, with regard to your former way of life, to put off your old self, which is being corrupted by its deceitful desires; to be made new in the attitude of your minds; and to put on the new self, created to be like God in true righteousness and holiness.

Therefore each of you must put off falsehood and speak truthfully to your neighbor, for we are all members of one body. In your anger do not sin: Do not let the sun go down while you are still angry, and do not give the devil a

> **foothold. Anyone who has been stealing must steal no longer, but must work, doing something useful with their own hands, that they may have something to share with those in need.**
>
> **Do not let any unwholesome talk come out of your mouths, but only what is helpful for building others up according to their needs, that it may benefit those who listen. And do not grieve the Holy Spirit of God, with whom you were sealed for the day of redemption. Get rid of all bitterness, rage and anger, brawling and slander, along with every form of malice. Be kind and compassionate to one another, forgiving each other, just as in Christ God forgave you.'**

Ephesians 5:1–2 (NIV) exhorts us further, **'Follow God's example, therefore, as dearly loved children and walk in the way of love, just as Christ loved us and gave himself up for us as a fragrant offering and sacrifice to God.'**

How wonderful! This is the knowledge that renews our understanding of this painful world and restores hope in our lives. We were raised from our sleep [spiritual death], much like Jesus was raised from the dead, to come alive in Christ and embrace a life of truth and righteousness, fully devoted to God and His people.

God's purpose for us whom He foreknew is that we be *conformed* to the image of His Son, Jesus! We are looking into a mirror—holding ourselves up against the perfect example of Christ. As we examine our hearts, thoughts, and actions in the light of His life, the Holy Spirit reveals where we fall short, gently guiding us to repent, correct, and align ourselves with His ways. This mirror doesn't condemn us; it shapes us, transforming our character so that we increasingly reflect Christ in every aspect of our lives.

This purpose of ours has been from when the world began.

Ephesians 2:10 (NIV):
10 For we are God's handiwork, created in Christ Jesus to do GOOD WORKS, which God prepared in advance for us to do.

Good works are not those deeds done out of obligation or for personal gain. They're not those actions that appear good on the outside but are motivated by wicked intentions. Good works are deeds that please God. They are such thoughts and actions that bear the fruits of righteousness to the glory of our Father, reflecting the nature of Christ, and they include, especially, those mundane details of ordinary living. Even in eating and drinking, we must glorify God.

Jesus, in **John 15**, describes Himself as the true vine. He makes it clear that we cannot bear these good fruits apart from Him, just as a branch cannot bear fruit if it does not abide in its vine.

Jesus is not only our access to God and the door through which we enter, but He is also the way and the path we are to continually walk in. He is the model of our faith.

By examining the life of the Son, we can understand what kind of children God desires us to be. **'For you did not receive the spirit of slavery to fall back into fear, but you have received the Spirit of adoption as sons, by whom we cry, "Abba! Father!" The Spirit himself bears witness with our spirit that we are children of God, and if children, then heirs—heirs of God and fellow heirs with Christ, provided we suffer with him in order that we may also be glorified with him' (Romans 8:15–17 ESV).**

In our context, a word like 'heir' can paint *pretty* pictures of greatness and even material enjoyment. While we do have a great inheritance in Christ beyond the material, we also see that, in the same verse above, our heirship is conditioned on suffering with Christ! Our call is to take up our cross, whatever that may look like, and follow Him.

In **Matthew 20**, the mother of James and John, the sons of Zebedee, may have had this in mind when she asked the Lord Jesus to allow her sons to sit at His left and right in His coming kingdom. Jesus responds by highlighting a very crucial element of Christianity: whoever desires to be great must serve, just as He did not come to be served but to serve.

The reality of this cross must have eventually hit the disciples, as many of them were persecuted, even killed, for their belief in Jesus. Many today (for example, in Northern Nigeria, parts of Asia, and elsewhere) still face persecution and death for their faith in Jesus. For some, it may look different: it could mean letting go of a job because it does not honour God or enduring public ridicule for your faith in Christ.

Whatever the case may be, our works must reflect our Lord.

The disciples of Jesus once asked Him what commandment was the greatest. His answer? **"'You shall love the Lord your God with all your heart and with all your soul and with all your mind. This is the great and first commandment. And a second is like it: You shall love your neighbor as yourself. On these two commandments depend all the Law and the Prophets'" (Matthew 22:37–40 ESV).**

What Jesus is saying here is that if we can do these two things, we are fulfilling every Law of God. Every other law is simply an extension of these two laws.

TAKING FROM THIS, reflecting Jesus can be split into two broad categories:

Fellowship with Him: Reflecting Christ means having a persistent desire to always be in communion with God in the fellowship of His Word and in prayer. We pray and study the Bible to know Him more, to be more like Him, to constantly be transformed into His image, like Adam, before sin distorted it, but now with a better Adam to follow, Christ. We study the Bible to receive discipline and correct doctrine, and to discern false prophets from true ones. We study the Bible to grow in our knowledge of God and to teach this truth to others so that they might be saved, for how will people hear without a preacher? Through the Word, we can give a defence for our hope in Christ **(Romans 10:17; 1 Peter 3:15).**

As our lover, our desire should be for Him: to sit at His feet and be with Him, just as we naturally long to be in the presence and company of those we love.

Jesus was one with God. He was never out of fellowship with God. Even as a young boy, He was found in His Father's house, listening and asking questions about the Scriptures. He prioritised Scripture in everything, often quoting it and pointing to its real-time fulfilment by His actions.

So intimate was the bond between Father and Son that in sadness or rejoicing, in weakness or in strength, Jesus always sought His Father in prayer, remaining faithful to God's will—trusting and obeying His Father at all times **(John 17:21; John 10:30; Luke 2:49; Matthew 26:39).** We are called to do the same.

In the story of Mary and Martha, Mary chose to sit at Jesus' feet while Martha was preoccupied with hospitality. Jesus praised Mary because she chose what was *good*—that which would not be taken from her. By the wisdom of God, we too must make those choices that constantly bring us to the feet of Christ to behold His face. Rather than being legalistic and striving to keep every law, all we need to do is look to Christ in fellowship with Him so that we may be as He is.

Furthermore, nothing uplifts the soul—humbling the mind and simultaneously expanding it—like meditating on God.

> *'There is something exceedingly improving to the mind in a contemplation of divinity—the science of Christ and Him crucified and the knowledge of the Godhead in the glorious Trinity. It is a subject so vast that all our thoughts are lost in its immensity—so deep that our pride is drowned in its infinity. There is in contemplating Christ a balm for every wound. In considering the Father, there is a comfort for every grief, and in the influence of the Holy Spirit there is a salve for every sore.'*[1]

Fellowship with others: God is Trinity, and He created us for fellowship with one another. As God said of Adam in the beginning, before creating Eve from his rib, it is also not good for Christians to be alone.

Christians are referred to as the body of Christ. Like a physical body, the body of Christ (the church) has members who are unified by being members of one body. How, then, can a member of a body be isolated? How can a member say, *'I am better off by myself?'* An isolated Christian is in dangerous waters because, as Christians, our strength is in God and in each other, just like the strength of the body is in the unity of the body. Once parts of the body become dismembered, it is no longer a body, and even individual parts lose their strength. The Bible strictly warns us not to neglect fellowship with other Christians **(Hebrews 10:25; 1 Corinthians 12:12–27)**. Wasn't even Jesus usually in the company of His disciples?

In Paul's letter to the Philippians, he admonishes them to have the same mind as Christ, **'who, though he was in**

1. Culled from Charles Spurgeon's notes on Malachi 3:6.

the form of God, did not count equality with God a thing to be grasped, but emptied himself, by taking the form of a servant, being born in the likeness of men. And being found in human form, he humbled himself by becoming obedient to the point of death, even death on a cross. Therefore God has highly exalted him and bestowed on him the name that is above every name' (Philippians 2:6–9, ESV).

Things are *reversed* in the Kingdom of God. While the world's rulers lord it over their subjects, the *great* Christian is the one who serves **(Matthew 20:25–28).**

Christ expressed the highest point of love and servanthood by laying down His life in obedience to His Father **(Philippians 2:8).** In the same way, we are called to lay down our lives for one another in love. For if we do not love the people we see, how can we love God whom we have not seen? **(1 John 4:20).** Jesus Himself said that an identifying mark of His disciples would be the love they showed for one another! **(John 13:35).**

We must endeavour to see people not merely according to the flesh, ranking them by their material estate, but as they are in Christ **(2 Corinthians 5:16)**—new creatures maturing in the likeness of their Creator. When we encounter others, we have to remember that we are not just engaging with personalities, temperaments, or flaws; we are encountering fellow image-bearers of God, and opportunities to practise love, patience, forgiveness, and humility. People and relationships are God's training ground for Christness.

Paul, in **1 Thessalonians 2:8 & 17**, reveals the depth of Christian love and relational commitment. He writes that he and his companions were delighted to share not only the Gospel but also their very lives, because the believers had become so dear to them. Their ministry was not transactional or distant; it was deeply personal, marked by affection, sacrifice, and shared life. When Paul was separated from them, he described it as being torn away, expressing intense longing and effort to see them again. These verses, and so many others in the Scriptures, show that Christian fellowship is not optional or superficial; it is a sharing of life and a mutual giving of selves, rooted in love and sustained by Christ Himself, the head over the body.

True fellowship with the saints is marked by a deep love and care for one another's souls in Christ, such that we cannot help but—like Paul—share our entire lives that they also be our glory and joy when Jesus comes **(1 Thessalonians 2:19–20)**, for our relationships carry eternal weight. In this way, fellowship is not merely companionship in the present, but an investment in one another's eternal destiny; being accountable and praying for each other **(James 5:16)**; bearing one another's burdens and restoring each other when we fall into sin **(Galatians 6:1)**, just as family looks out for family—are we not the family of God?

Our Christian fellowship is one that should inflame our love for God. It should contain those conversations that deepen our love for God and provoke a deeper longing to serve Him—not to show off our devotion, but to encourage our supply to each other in love.

Just as Israel was called out of the nations to be God's inheritance, Christ has called us out of darkness to be His people, for Israel was a type of the Church (**1 Kings 8:51–53**). We are a covenant people called to reflect God's holiness.

Although we are commanded to prioritise our brethren, our duty to love extends beyond our fellow believers to everyone around us—neighbours and enemies included **(Galatians 6:10).**

As we lay down our lives for others, we grow in love and maturity—we conform to Christ (**Ephesians 4:13–24**).

IT WAS PROPHESIED about Jesus that '**... to Him shall be the obedience of the peoples' (Genesis 49:10, AMP).** Through His sacrifice for us, when we believe, our lives turn around in seconds, enabling us to do the things we couldn't do before.

There is a power that translates men from death to life **(Ephesians 1:18–20).** A power that, when it comes upon a man, eliminates the desire to do evil and makes him give up everything in obedience to Christ. A good example of this is Paul: when he encountered Jesus, there was nothing more to be said. The change was radical!

By the power of God, we can reflect Christ. Let us!

Once Saved, Always Saved

The idea of '*once saved, always saved,*' so far, would seem to pose more danger to the Christian community than good. Its core message is that once a person is saved, they are *forever* saved—eternally secure—and that God cannot revoke His gift of salvation, no matter how much a believer intentionally dabbles, and even remains, in unrepentant sin.

Hm. It worries me.

The *'once saved, always saved'* theology seems to promote a Christianity that is careless in guarding its greatest treasure: salvation. It seems to paint a picture of ingratitude and aloofness from the very core of our faith, Jesus.

The Bible assures us of the security of our salvation in Christ. We are predestined, regenerated, and justified by Him. Salvation is a sovereign act of God, where He renews us and gives us a new heart capable of truly serving Him. As Jonathan Edwards rightly put it, we *'contribute nothing to salvation except the sin that made it necessary.'* As such, it is not such a thing that we can *lose* like one loses a piece of jewellery **(Romans 8:30–34; Titus 3:5).** Jesus assures us that nobody can snatch us out of His hand **(John 10:28)**—and what mighty hands He has; the same hands that fashioned this world out of nothingness and holds all things together. Nothing can take us from His hands. *Nothing.*

While it is true that we cannot lose our salvation in that sense of carelessly misplacing an item, another truth is that every moment we do not spend getting *closer to* Jesus, we drift *farther* from Him until we no longer recognise the salvation we claim, and bear little difference from those who are not saved.

What happens to the branch that does not abide in the vine? It becomes barren; it withers and is thrown into the fire to be burned **(John 15:6).** In **Revelation 3:14–22,** God, speaking to the church in Laodicea, warns them to repent from their lukewarmness, lest He would spit them out of His mouth.

Do we *really* want to be spat out of the Lord's mouth? What is spat out but that which is foul-tasting and undesirable?

Salvation is characterised by our growing similarities to God, as His children, with the help of the Holy Spirit, until **'... Christ be formed in you' (Galatians 4:19, KJV).** To be saved and to love God means we do not constantly try to dance around the line that brings us just *close enough* to light and just *far enough* from darkness.

Why would we choose to be wicked toward God, who has shown us such immeasurable kindness? See what Christ has done for us! Our entire lives would never be enough to bless His Name for His marvellous works in our lives. But we must give them, for that's all that we have. We already have such a paltry gift for the King, yet we still want to negotiate? What morbid villainy.

Jesus said, **'If you [really] love Me, you will keep and obey My commandments' (John 14:15, AMP).** In light of this, we reflect God when we obey Him. Our intimacy with God is not only a matter of unrestrained tears and emotions, but it also looks more like a nearness wrought through commitment and obedience.

We have a commitment to God; let us not try to have our cake and eat it too. We cannot reach for salvation with one hand and hold on to sin with the other. It is like playing with fire if we choose to linger near the fence, instead of going deeper with God by progressing on the Narrow Way.

James 4:4 clearly warns us, friendship with the world

is enmity with God. What else tempts us but our own [evil] desire for the [evil] things of the world? And what can the world offer that does not ultimately end in death?

We have been set free for a reason.

Ephesians 5:16–17 (AMP):
16 making the very most of your time [on earth, recognizing and taking advantage of each opportunity and using it with wisdom and diligence], because the days are [filled with] evil.
17 Therefore do not be foolish and thoughtless, but understand and firmly grasp what the will of the Lord is.

LET US NOT BE FOOLISH.

Let us not be thoughtless.

Let us love the Lord with the best of our being.

Let us not desire or idolise what the Lord has delivered us from.

What About Your Weaknesses?

On the topic of our weaknesses and inhibitions, it helps to remember one thing every time they pop up: God has already made provisions for your weaknesses. These provisions—His mercies—are our fail-safe.

As long as we live in the world and in our frail bodies, there will always be that battle between what God wants and what our flesh wants. **Galatians 5:17 (CSB)** puts it well, **'For the flesh desires what is against the Spirit, and the Spirit desires what is against the flesh; these are opposed to each other, so that you don't do what you want.'**

But here is some better news: **Hebrews 10:14 (NLT)** says, **'For by that one offering he forever made perfect those who are being made holy.'** He has made *perfect* those who are *being* made holy! You have *been* imputed with the perfection of Jesus, whom you have accepted as your Savior, your justification is sealed—impossible to be added to. However, you are *being* made holy ... meaning that your sanctification is an ongoing process!

Note these two things:

First, Jesus, by His sacrifice, has killed you and replaced you with Himself—His kind of life. That part that you could not do, the nature of sin that you could not resist and which made you prone to sin, He has taken that away for you by His blood. He has done the heavy lifting.

Second, the other part of this equation is what you must now do. You must be sanctified daily until the perfect day when Jesus returns for you.

While you are at once saved when you believe in the atoning work of Jesus Christ, your mind, emotions, feelings, etc., need some serious transformation. Those changes occur as we consistently yield to the Holy Spirit —who guides us into truth—so we come into alignment with God's will for our lives.

Romans 12:2 (AMP) says:
'And do not be conformed to this world [any
longer with its superficial values and

> **customs], but be transformed and progressively changed [as you mature spiritually] by the RENEWING of your mind [focusing on godly values and ethical attitudes], so that you may prove [for yourselves] what the will of God is, that which is good and acceptable and perfect [in His plan and purpose for you].'**

It is by renewing our minds, by focusing on godly values and attitudes, that we transform our thinking. God has done His part, but this renewal is also our responsibility. We must be sober and alert. Practical examples include watching the kinds of material that we consume, from movies, music and social media to other content that does not edify. Others include watching our associations and friendships to ensure the people surrounding us do not enhance our conformity to the world but to the Word.

Shall we dine with Jesus in the morning, then sit with scoffers at noon?

But what happens when your weaknesses show up (as they surely will)? What happens when you fail or falter in this process of renewing your mind?

What happens is **Hebrews 4:16 (NLT): 'So let us come boldly to the throne of our gracious God. There we will receive his mercy, and we will find grace to help us when we need it most.'** You do nobody but Satan a favour by wallowing in the guilt of your sin. Repent and start over!

The understanding that the victory of Jesus deals with our obligation to sin is very crucial to our identity as believers. From Adam, we became slaves to sin, but in Jesus, we receive freedom from our obligation to sin **(Romans 8:1–2)**. This means that we have power over sin; we can keep God's commandments because we love Him.

This, therefore, is the distinction between an unbeliever and one who is saved:

A person who has not come into Christ possesses a sinful nature that is, in a sense, their master. They are obligated to sin. To sin is very normal to their makeup because they do not know Christ. A rough analogy: Think of a fish in water, its obligation is to swim. It cannot help but swim. What is abnormal is a fish walking on land. When an unbeliever does something *good*, he is actually acting against his nature, and even the good is often tainted by sin, selfishness, and unrighteousness. An unbeliever cannot please God because their very nature is in contradiction to God's holy nature.

When you understand this, you'll see that in sin, we never *really* had free will, because we had no choice but to sin—it was our only option. True freedom of choice only existed in a relationship with God, the good King. The sole reason why Adam could choose to disobey God was that he was still connected to God—he could obey or disobey. After the Fall, that freedom was lost because, unlike God, sin is a brutal master who cages our free will. Sin became our default nature, our only mode of operation.

If you think this to be false, ask yourself why God had to rescue you before you could be translated into His Kingdom of Light. *Could you have reached for Him if He didn't reach for you? Did you really have free will? When you tried to stop that addiction with the sheer power of your will, were you able to?*

On the flip side, for one who believes, they receive the life of Christ, which is a new nature that has the capacity to resist sin. Jesus Christ kills that rebellion inherent in all born of Adam by giving us a new heart that desires not to sin but to please God. This is why the believer has no obligation to sin. Instead, our duty is to please God **(1 John 3:9)**.

Think again of that fish in water, but imagine that it isn't actually a fish but a tadpole. Unlike a fish, a tadpole can develop into a frog that can live both on land and in water. However, for us—unlike a typical frog—our new nature means that we can not only choose to stay on land (in Christ), rather than return to water (sin), but also that we actually, progressively, lose the desire to swim, and that one perfect day, we will never have to swim again! As the Word says, **'But the path of the just is as the shining light, That shineth more and more unto the perfect day' (Proverbs 4:18, KJV).**

Several times in Scripture, we see Jesus use the phrase, ***'go and sin no more'*** during His ministry, like in **John 8** when He forgave the woman caught in adultery. Such a statement is not just a command; it is a Spirit–filled empowerment that rids the receiver of the desire to continue in sin, having experienced the One without sin!

Now, this does not mean that our sinful nature (the flesh) will not rear its ugly head. The water will keep calling the frog to swim in it. The flesh keeps fighting the Spirit, an internal battle like Paul woefully cries out about in **Romans 7**.

Spurgeon puts it well:

'The position of sin in a natural man is that of a king on his throne; the position of sin in a Christian is that of a bandit hiding in secret places trying to get back its old usurped dominion but failing in the attempt.'

What, then, is our consolation?

Proverbs 24:16 (NLT) says, **'The godly may trip seven times, but they will get up again.'** The life of a believer is marked, not by perfection, but by daily confession and repentance because sin is not normal for the Christian and must be done away with so we become more like Christ.

Making mistakes is called *failing forward*, as long as we get up again. When a child stumbles as he tries to walk, is the child condemned and told never to try walking again? Or is he encouraged to try again? Of course, it is the latter! How much more we, babes in Christ?

Like Samuel said to the Israelites, **'Do not be afraid. You have [indeed] done all this evil; yet do not turn away from following the Lord, but serve the Lord with all your heart' (1 Samuel 12:20, AMP).**

We miss the point when we think that we have to be perfect to be in Christ or to be in His body, the Church. Jesus said it Himself, **'It is not those who are healthy who need a physician, but [only] those who are sick. I did not come to call the [self-proclaimed] righteous [who see no need to repent], but sinners to repentance [to change their old way of thinking, to turn from sin and to seek God and His righteousness]' (Luke 5:31–32, AMP).**

If the Word says that you can emulate God **(Ephesians**

5:1) and be perfect like Him **(Matthew 5:48)**, then shun every tongue that makes you feel like it will always be a struggle to do so—the believer does not live life anticipating sin, like he is helpless against it. In truth, you only need to start looking at God and *thinking* like Him in terms of possibilities, so that you can come to the reality of the fact. Has His divine power not given us all we need for godly living? God does not lie. We must believe Him.

If you've ever tried to pull a surprise on someone, you have to think like that person to ensure they do not find out about the surprise beforehand. You have to get into their minds to predict what they may or may not do, and this is only possible because of the knowledge you have of them. In the same way, we can think like God because we have the mind of Christ! By looking at Him through unbroken fellowship with Him, in Word and in prayer, we can know what God likes and dislikes (His thoughts and character), and emulate Him in our daily living. We can *try*.

The good news is that every step we take in Christ, we do so with the help of the Holy Spirit. It is when we walk in the Spirit that we do not fulfil the desires of the flesh. **Galatians 5:16 & 25 (AMP)** says: **'But I say, walk habitually in the [Holy] Spirit [seek Him and be responsive to His guidance], and then you will certainly not carry out the desire of the sinful nature [which responds impulsively without regard for God and His precepts]. If we [claim to] live by the [Holy] Spirit, we must also walk by the Spirit [with personal integrity, godly character, and moral courage—our conduct empowered by the Holy Spirit].'**

By responding to the Spirit's guidance, we become more mature in Christ, so we do not remain babies in Him forever. The Bible is not supportive of Christians staying as babies rather than maturing.

I love how **Ephesians 4:14–16** puts it in the **MSG** translation:

> **'NO PROLONGED INFANCIES AMONG US, PLEASE. We'll not tolerate babes in the woods, small children who are easy prey for predators. God wants us to grow up, to know the whole truth and tell it in love—like Christ in everything. We take our lead from Christ, who is the source of everything we do. He keeps us in step with each other. His very breath and blood flow through us, nourishing us so that we will grow up healthy in God, robust in love.**

We are to grow and deepen in our knowledge of Christ, so we look more like Him. This growth happens only when we intentionally seek it through fellowship with God. Beholding Him unwaveringly is what transforms us! Remember **John 15**? The flip side of the branch that does not abide is the branch that **does** abide—this is the branch that bears fruit!

Proverbs 24:10 says that if a person falls in the day of adversity, then their strength is small. It is by continuously beholding God, building up ourselves in the Word and in prayer, that we're able to withstand trials and temptations that the world throws at us to test our faith.

You reap what you sow. If you sow to the flesh, then you reap the same. If you sow to the Spirit, you reap the same **(Galatians 6:8)**. Practically, you cannot spend five minutes praying and over five hours scrolling through social media daily and expect to be spiritually strengthened or mature as time goes on.

Sow to the spirit; do the things that please God, whether big or small, and exercise yourself in godliness **(1 Timothy 4:7)** to build your spiritual stamina, then watch your strength grow! Spend time praying, spend time reading your Bible and sound Christian literature, and fellowship often with other Christians. Mount guardrails around your soul by maintaining a lifestyle that keeps the world at bay.

What we race for is an imperishable prize **(1 Corinthians 9)**. If earthly athletes can train obsessively, giving their all, for a material prize, how much more we, who race for an eternal prize? It is worth everything it will cost us. As our Lord once asked, is it not better to enter the Kingdom of Heaven maimed, than with our whole bodies intact be candidates of hell?

Regardless of our many earthly woes and temptations, Christ is our assurance. Let us depend wholly on Him '... **who is able to keep you from stumbling and to present you blameless before the presence of his glory with great joy' (Jude 1:24, ESV)**.

Knowing this, it is safe to say that, like Paul, we can indeed glory in our weaknesses! For it is in our weakness that His strength rests upon us **(2 Corinthians 12:9)**.

Ideally, we should not sin. We must hate our sins deeply and not endorse them in any way [by confessing them]—sometimes, we are tempted to do so when God mercifully brings good out of our evil actions, as He often does. We must strive for perfection. We must press forward to be better every day, to look more like God every day, for He is the standard. And what a high standard!

However, Christ remains our advocate when we do sin, as we surely will **(1 John 2:1–2)**. In fact, if we say we have no sin, then we make God a liar **(1 John 1:8–9)**. When we confess our sins He forgives us, beckoning us into the Father's presence as we stand on His merit **(Hebrews 4:16)**. And even when we bemoan our frail constituency, thinking that we should have *known better*; even when our hearts still condemn us, tempting us to hold on to false guilt [which is a kind of self-pride that leads to despair and a desire to pay by ourselves for our sins, thus rendering Christ's sacrifice inefficient, for godly sorrow leads to repentance not self-judgement] after we have confessed and been forgiven, God is greater than our hearts **(1 John 3:20–22)**. He does not regard us any less—for to do so would be to regard Christ, the One who stands before us, as such.

When we sin, sometimes we *fall our own hand*[2]. But that is not the most important hand we have fallen. We must remember that it is God we first sin against, and then the people directly affected by the sin we committed —referencing the order of the two greatest commandments. It is from there we must start to make restitution, and when we reach ourselves once more, we will find out that we easily make peace with our souls when we have made peace with God and men.

---

2. Nigerian Pidgin English which means failing to meet set expectations.

When we wallow, we rob God even more. Think of a housekeeper who, whilst preparing the house for a dinner, breaks a precious plate. What is better: to sit and bemoan the plate, stopping all dinner preparations and costing his master even more time and resources when the master arrives and finds no food? Or to quickly clean up the mess, make alternative dinner plans, and confess to his master when he arrives? The punishment would certainly be worse if the master had to remain hungry! The best way to repay what we owe is to carry on in the service of our Master.

Proverbs 16:6 (NIV):
Through love and faithfulness sin is atoned for;
through the fear of the Lord evil is avoided.

His mercy is greater than our mistakes. We can be of good cheer, then, for Jesus has overcome the world!

A Father's Discipline

Since Christ stands for us, God sees us as perfect, and Christ's pure blood pleads and continually speaks for us, appeasing God's wrath forever.

God sees us as holy, then, even as we are progressively sanctified **(Hebrews 10:14).**

As a response to Christ's sacrifice, we are to put on Christ, so we do not heed the flesh's desires and, thus, grieve the Holy Spirit **(Romans 13:14; Ephesians 4:30).** We are called to **'purify ourselves as He is pure' (1 John 3:3);**

what this means is that we have a role to play—we have to fight the good fight of faith **(1 Timothy 6:12)**.

However, at times we fail to purify ourselves; we err, as expected **(1 John 1:8–9)**. One of the ways that God redeems us is through discipline. This discipline can be active or passive:

Through *chastisement*: God often chastises us through discipline to restore us to Himself. A good example of this active chastisement can be seen in **1 Corinthians 11**, where some believers took Holy Communion in an unworthy manner and became weak and sick as a result. Another well-known example is how God would often hand the Israelites over to their enemies as covenant discipline to draw them back to Himself.

Through *trials*: God can also use difficult times to prune us. A clear example is the thorn in Paul's flesh. Though it was from the devil, God permitted it to keep Paul from becoming conceited **(2 Corinthians 12)**.

Hebrews 12:7–11 (ESV) says:

It is for discipline that you have to endure. God is treating you as sons. For what son is there whom his father does not discipline? If you are left without discipline, in which all have participated, then you are illegitimate children and not sons. Besides this, we have had earthly fathers who disciplined us and we respected them. Shall we not much more be subject to the Father of spirits and live? For they disciplined us for a short time as it

> **seemed best to them, but he disciplines us for our good, that we may share his holiness. For the moment all discipline seems painful rather than pleasant, but later it yields the peaceful fruit of righteousness to those who have been trained by it.**

God's love is designed to drive us to perfection. We are transformed into His image because of His love for us—His love communicates this perfect vision of what we could be, and He takes us by the hand, never letting go, to get there.

Take Gideon, for example, who referred to himself as **'the least'** in his father's house during a difficult time in Israel. When the Angel of the Lord appeared to him, he was called a **'mighty man of valour' (Judges 6:12).** Would you look at that! A man who still went on to lay out a fleece twice, just to be doubly sure that God was leading him.

Love believes the best, and this is how God sees us. The evidence is endless. Even when we were sinners, He saw who we could be in Christ.

> **Ephesians 2:4–5 (ESV):**
> **But God, being rich in mercy, because of the great love with which he loved us, even when we were dead in our trespasses, made us alive together with Christ—by grace you have been saved—**

God's discipline is not Him punishing us, in that

retributive sense, for our wrongdoings, because His wrath was exhausted upon Christ on the cross **(Romans 5:8; 8:1)** and so no condemnation remains for us; it is on those who do not believe that God's wrath remains **(John 3:36)**. Our debt has been paid, so God remembers the believer's sins no more **(Hebrews 8:12)**. Even though God often allows the natural consequences of our sinful actions to occur, He uses them for our own good—a far greater good than we can imagine in the present.

We must embrace God's discipline no matter what shape it takes; whatever the form, we can be sure that we will look more like Him in the end.

Let us be like the Psalmist who says, **'It is good for me that I have been afflicted; That I might learn thy statutes' (Psalm 119:71, KJV).**

> **'For a command is a lamp, teaching is a light, and corrective discipline is the way to life' (Proverbs 6:23, CSB).**

Our affliction is good if it drives us to His embrace!

HALLELUJAH!

Good News!

How are we righteous in the sight of God? Not by anything we do, but by believing in the work of Christ on the cross, His righteousness is imputed to us **(Romans 4:5)**.

Jesus came to fix our hearts. He gives us a new heart, a heart of flesh, according to God's promise **(Ezekiel 36:26).**

What a soft heart does is that it moves us easily to surrender and repentance.

It is a heart that wants to please God, no matter how many times it fails.

It is a heart that yearns for the will of God to be done, regardless of the cost.

It is a heart that transcends the hardness and weaknesses of the flesh because God dwells in it.

17

SALT AND LIGHT

Salt and Light, representative of the believer, are preserving influences upon this world.
—Maranatha

I once read a book, *In His Steps: What Would Jesus Do?* by Charles Sheldon. It narrated the story of a group of Christians who, after a significant [kinda scandalous] incident at their small town church, resolved to act in every circumstance as they believed Jesus would if He were in that situation.

This is what it means to look at God to look like Him. We go to this Mirror and take a good look at ourselves, but not to see *just* ourselves. We behold God **(2 Corinthians 3:18)**, and we begin to reflect Him, giving off His light to all and sundry.

When James likens a man who knows the Word of God without obeying it to someone who studies his reflection carefully and then forgets what he looks like once he looks away **(James 1:23–24)**, he calls to mind the life of many believers today who have *head knowledge* without *heart knowledge*. They come to this Mirror (The Word, Jesus), look at it and see not just themselves but the One they should look like —God—but they do not apply this knowledge to their lives, so it is taken away from them once they look away. Much like the rocky ground in the parable of the sower **(Matthew 13)**.

The idea of salt and light brings to mind a preservation that would not be possible without these elements. Salt preserves from decay, and light preserves from darkness. This is who the believer becomes in Christ, a preserving element of the world.

> **2 Corinthians 2:14–16 (NIV)** puts it better:
> **14 But thanks be to God, who always leads us as captives in Christ's triumphal procession and uses us to spread the aroma of the knowledge of him everywhere.**
> **15 For we are to God the pleasing aroma of Christ among those who are being saved and those who are perishing.**
> **16 To the one we are an aroma that brings death; to the other, an aroma that brings life. And who is equal to such a task?**

Apostle Paul in **1 Corinthians 3:3–4 (CSB)** admonishes the Corinthian church to rise above mere humanity, being like people of the world. This is a superior calling that is not without responsibilities.

It is easy to be in the world. In fact, without much thought or intentionality in Christian living, believers can find themselves conformed to the world. But it is a holy standard we are called to; let us not settle for less.

The taste of salt is very distinct and hard to miss. The presence of light in a dark room, even just a flicker, cannot go unnoticed. This is who the Christian is called to be in light of our new belief in Jesus.

In Matthew 5:13–16 (NIV), Jesus says:

13 You are the salt of the earth. But if the salt loses its saltiness, how can it be made salty again? It is no longer good for anything, except to be thrown out and trampled underfoot.

14 You are the light of the world. A town built on a hill cannot be hidden.

15 Neither do people light a lamp and put it under a bowl. Instead they put it on its stand, and it gives light to everyone in the house.

16 In the same way, let your light shine before others, that they may see your GOOD DEEDS and glorify your Father in heaven.

We have Christ, but it is not just for the betterment of our lives and that of our immediate loved ones. Jesus has a purpose to which He has called us. He has called us to shine and direct all attention back to Him so that even more people may find Him and be reconciled to the Father.

Becoming salt and light requires a constant process of refinement. In **Mark 9:49**, Jesus says that every sacrifice will be salted with fire. He speaks here in reference to the Old Testament practices of seasoning animal and grain sacrifices with salt **(Leviticus 2:13; Ezekiel 43:24)**. In light of the New Covenant with God through Jesus, we know that animal sacrifices no longer apply. Rather, we are the living sacrifices **(Romans 12:1)** called to willingly offer our lives to God, continually seasoned and refined by the fire of the Holy Spirit, so that we grow in sanctification, holiness and resemblance to God. It is through this refining work of the Spirit that we gain the ability to *season* and *illuminate* the lives of others.

We must grasp the depth of the Christian's call to preserve the world to understand what God has called us to be and to do. What does a meal without salt taste like? What does a room without light look like? All other qualities can only be appreciated through the presence of salt or light.

Noah, in his time, was salt. The moment he and his family entered the ark, the flood began **(Genesis 7:11–13)**. The Bible also prophesies the rapture, a day that is coming very soon, when Jesus will return to gather His people unto Himself. Without us, believers, the world would implode!

Luke 17:26–27 (CSB):
'Just as it was in the days of Noah, so it will be in the days of the Son of Man: People went on

> **eating, drinking, marrying and being given in marriage until the day Noah boarded the ark, and the flood came and destroyed them all.'**

Just like that day, **'the heavens shall pass away with a great noise, and the elements shall melt with fervent heat, the earth also and the works that are therein shall be burned up' (2 Peter 3:10, KJV).**

That day will be the day of God's judgement. **'Let no one deceive you with empty arguments, for God's wrath is coming on the disobedient because of these things' (Ephesians 5:6, CSB).**

As we have been reconciled to God, He entrusts to us His ministry of reconciliation—appealing to others who are lost through us—so that we may help bring in the lost, that they may not perish **(2 Corinthians 5:18–20)**. We do this by *being* salt and light—by remembering what we look like.

Jesus never asked us to become salt or light. In **Matthew 5:14**, He simply says that we are. This means we are either living up to that responsibility or failing at it through our actions or inactions. The believer who is afraid to stand out, or to stand up for what they believe as Jesus calls us to, is like the salt in **Matthew 5:13** that has lost its taste. Of what use is it? We can never affect the world for Jesus by becoming like the world. If we fail to stand out, we are of no use.

'Let your light so shine before men ...' The purpose of light is to illuminate and make visible what is around it.

For light to expose, it must first itself be exposed. If it is hidden in any way, it becomes useless.

We cannot selectively shine, then. We cannot be vocal about Christ only in church or among fellow believers, for it is those who do not know Christ who need Him the most.

When we hide Christ, we do a disservice to both the kingdom of God and to the world. When we remain silent on a matter because *it doesn't concern us,'* we withhold the truth from those who need to hear it. The text says that the candle gives light to **'all that are in the house,'** reminding us that the message of Christ is for everyone. All our neighbours.

Yet we do not act autonomously; we do not own ourselves. We have a Lord—the Lord—and we *only* go where He sends us, doing only *what* He asks us to. Sometimes, our desires may seem good, but it is God alone who can give us what is truly good. Take Paul, for example, who wanted to evangelise in certain locations but was prevented by the Holy Ghost from entering those places **(Acts 16:6–7)**. Let us be responsive to God's leading. He does it best, for He knows best.

In light of this, we must also be careful to shine *how* God wants us to, for our King determines both the means and the end in our service of Him. We must not project our own ambitions onto God or use the Gospel as a cover.

Whatever ideas we have, whatever actions we wish to take, we must ask ourselves:

Will this make people look at God, or will it make people look at me?

Will I, in the end, be more conformed to Christ?

Will gazes be lifted heavenward, or will sights be cast down toward the material?

Let us be the ones having holy conversations, speaking words that uplift men and glorify God. Let us not be the ones using idle words and laughing at crude jokes that undermine our Christian faith. Let us be people who make others look *up*. Let us not be those who cannot give a defence for the hope that we have, but make a mockery of Christianity just by our ignorance and the way we live.

Let us be haters of sin and friends of God. Let us not be double-minded, trying to tango with the world from time to time. Let us be sober and alert, redeeming the time and taking hold of that for which Christ has taken hold of us—eternal life. Let us not be slothful in our endeavours or earthly-minded, so unduly attached to the things of the world that thoughts of Heaven bring no joy to our hearts. Let us be the ones praying to the Lord to send more labourers into His harvest—even as we labour in the Lord's work while it is day.

Remember, not perfection now but progressive sanctification—a process that will culminate in perfection when He comes.

If our hearts are for God, it will be evident in our dedication to the truth.

Every shortcoming, addiction, and bad habit—those we fear make us look like frauds or hypocrites—dies under the heat of Christ's holiness as we draw closer and closer to Him, **'for our God is a consuming fire' (Hebrews 12:29, CSB).**

'For you, God, tested us; you refined us as silver is refined' (Psalm 66:10, CSB).

The trick, therefore, is to get closer. The closer we are to the true Light, our eternal Monarch, the brighter we shine.

True influence is when our lives bring holy flavour and light to all those around us, so that the prophecy of **Zechariah 8:23 (CSB)** becomes the testimony of our lives: **'... in those days, ten men from nations of every language will grab the robe of a Jewish man tightly, urging: Let us go with you, for we have heard that God is with you.'**

MAY this be the testament of our lives, in Jesus' Name. Amen.

18

SOMEWHERE BETTER THAN EDEN

Spending my life here with You, preparing for the next with You.
—Maranatha

Did Adam pray? If he did, what did he pray for? The Bible tells us that God came in the cool of the evening to the garden of Eden to commune with Adam **(Genesis 3:8)**. While Scripture does not explicitly state how often this occurred, we can infer from God calling out to Adam that He expected regular fellowship with Him.

For Adam, communion and fellowship with God were a natural part of life. It might sound foreign, but prayer—which is essentially communication with God—is not merely a hotline for petitions. Rather, it is a dialogue between God and humanity, filled with thanksgiving, adoration and intimacy.

We were created for unbroken communion with God. In **Revelation 4**, we get a glimpse of Heaven, where its inhabitants never cease to adore and bless God. From our human, tainted perspective, this might seem like a bore—but newsflash: this is what life in Eden would have looked like. A life of unceasing worship and fellowship with God, expressed through every action, from work to rest!

Heaven on Earth

The New Covenant reveals something unique that I believe is often downplayed in our walk as 21st-century Christians.

When we look back at the Old Covenant, we see a consistency in how God calls His people to Himself—collectively. Just as He made a covenant with the Israelites of old, He now calls people from every nation and tribe, not just Israel, to be one people in Jesus, our Saviour and King; we are the Israel of God **(Revelation 5:9; Galatians 6:16)**.

There is a tendency we have to be individualistic about our faith, but this should not be so. It is not biblical. Right from when we are born, we are born into a family. When we are born again, we are also born into the family of God, united by the blood of Christ, which was shed for us.

This family is the church, first mentioned in **Matthew 16:18**, where Jesus declared that He would build His church and that it would not be overcome by the enemy.

The church is synonymous with the body of Christ, encompassing all who believe in the saving work of Jesus, who is also the head of the church **(Colossians 1:18).**

The Scriptures make it clear that we should not neglect the gathering of other Christians, but rather encourage one another, especially as the Second Coming of Christ draws near **(Hebrews 10:25).** This call goes beyond merely meeting physically with other believers on the Lord's Day; it is a command to commune with the body of Christ, to fellowship intimately with other blood-bought humans. There is a clause here that we often overlook—we are to do this, *especially* as we see the Day of the Lord (the Rapture) approaching. But why?

If you have ever had a toothache or even a common cold, you understand something about the mechanics of the body. A body is such a united entity that when the smallest part suffers, the entire body is affected. The Bible makes this clear.

1 Corinthians 12:22–26 (NIV):
22 On the contrary, those parts of the body that seem to be weaker are indispensable,
23 and the parts that we think are less honorable we treat with special honor. And the parts that are unpresentable are treated with special modesty,
24 while our presentable parts need no special treatment. But God has put the body together, giving greater honor to the parts that lacked it,
25 so that there should be no division in the

body, but that its parts should have equal concern for each other.

26 If one part suffers, every part suffers with it; if one part is honored, every part rejoices with it.

The unity of the body requires that each part *encourages* the others by functioning as it should—ears listening, heart pumping, legs walking. By faithfully playing their part, each member shows *concern* for the others. This mutual care is not merely for harmony; it leads to one ultimate end, which is the growth, flourishing, and maturity of the whole body.

Ephesians 4:11–16 (NIV):

11 So Christ himself gave the apostles, the prophets, the evangelists, the pastors and teachers,

12 to equip his people for works of service, so that the body of Christ may be built up

13 until we all reach unity in the faith and in the knowledge of the Son of God and become mature, attaining to the whole measure of the fullness of Christ.

14 Then we will no longer be infants, tossed back and forth by the waves, and blown here and there by every wind of teaching and by the cunning and craftiness of people in their deceitful scheming.

15 Instead, speaking the truth in love, we will

grow to become in every respect the mature
body of him who is the head, that is, Christ.
16 From him the whole body, joined and held
together by every supporting ligament, grows
and builds itself up in love, as each part does
its work.

From the foregoing, we can see that the growth of the body is directly tied to each part doing its work. This includes the work that Christ Himself does: giving the church apostles, prophets, evangelists, pastors, and teachers, as well as spiritual gifts **(1 Corinthians 12)**, and the sacraments of Baptism and Holy Communion. All of this is designed to help us grow in love, mature in faith, and increasingly conform to His image.

The work we do can be summed up in one word, then: participation. The notion that we can serve God from our bedrooms is very foreign to the Christian faith. Yes, our devotions are personal, but they are certainly not private.

We must participate in the body; we cannot be passengers. If we choose to sit on the sidelines—withholding our gifts, our time, our presence or our love—we deny others encouragement, support and growth. Sitting on the sidelines is not neutral; it diminishes the whole.

We must show concern for the body. We must pray for the body. When we desire spiritual gifts, it must be for the good of the body. We must love the body. It is in love that we are called to grow—not through any external accomplishments or works. Love is the identity by which the believer is known, not by wealth, position, or material success.

Remember the greatest commandment? To love God. And what is the second that is just like it? To love our neighbours as ourselves. The New Testament emphasises not just loving our neighbours, but prioritising our brethren **(Galatians 6:10)**. As Jesus said in **Matthew 12:46–50**, our true family are those who do the will of our Father in Heaven!

I have said all these to say that Heaven begins among us here, in the family of Christ—a place where we fellowship with God and with the saints (fellow believers). The church is the closest replica of Heaven. For in the church alone is Jesus the King, His statutes faithfully obeyed and His blessings most tangibly perceived.

Commenting on **Amos 3:3**, Spurgeon puts it like this:

> *'Like effects spring from like causes. All sinners are brethren in sin. Our walk evidences our heart. Those whom we walk with here, we must live with forever.'*

Think about it: if you really believe in Jesus, those you are most likely to meet in Heaven are your church members and all others in the body of Christ.

I cannot count how many times my heart has been lifted heavenward after a Sunday sermon, or a conversation or prayer with the saints. My prayer is that I may also restore my brethren's hearts in the same way. I've found that showing concern for others is a proven method of getting out of my own head, especially when the world provokes me to selfishness. And we need such encouragement, for it reminds us of our eternal destination when we forget, as we often do. We need such encouragement all the more because, all around us, the world unfailingly attempts to pull our gaze downward in countless ways.

No doubt, we will get hurt. Not only because false churches abound, but also because even true, biblical churches are made up of imperfect people who are still progressing in sanctification. But if God forgave us, who are we not to forgive? The biblical standard is clear: we must forgive our brethren not seven times, but seventy times seven times **(Matthew 18:21–22)**.

The mistake we often make, and that I have seen frequently, is compartmentalising our faith. Here is what I mean: you have a Christian who has *church* friends, and *work* friends, and many other categories of relationships, yet none of these friendships overlap. Why? Often because they believe their church friends won't *get* certain aspects of their life. What ends up happening, however, is that they begin to live double lives—behaving one way at church and another way at work, for example.

We need not live this way. Let us surround our souls with people who will safeguard them. Let us walk with those who share our faith. Let us not be afraid to open our hearts to those we are most likely to meet in Heaven—always with wisdom and discretion.

Nevertheless, this maturity we are reaching for will be fully realised when perfection comes **(1 Corinthians 13)**. In the meantime, we must continue to conform to Christ, the image of God, who is love.

Hebrews 6:10 (NIV):
God is not unjust; he will not forget your work

and the love you have shown him as you have helped his people and continue to help them.

Jesus is Coming Again ... Soon

The Bible speaks of a new Heaven and a new earth **(Revelation 21)**, a future marked by a painless, tearless, and deathless existence for humanity under the reign of King Jesus.

This is not an impersonal encounter, like all Christians will suddenly be transported to utopia. Scripture says that God Himself will wipe away our tears.

> **Revelation 21:3-4 (CSB):**
> **Then I heard a loud voice from the throne:**
> **"Look, God's dwelling is with humanity, and he will live with them. They will be his peoples, and God himself will be with them and will be their God. He will wipe away every tear from their eyes. Death will be no more; grief, crying, and pain will be no more, because the previous things have passed away."**

It will be a time of joy for all who choose Him as Lord; a world where wild animals will dwell in unity with domestic ones and even be led by a child **(Isaiah 11)**. Sounds familiar, doesn't it? Brings to mind when Adam named the animals in Eden.

Before this, Scripture teaches that there will be the rapture—the catching up of the saints to meet Christ in the air. '**For the Lord himself will descend from heaven**

with a shout, with the archangel's voice, and with the trumpet of God, and the dead in Christ will rise first. Then we who are still alive, who are left, will be caught up together with them in the clouds to meet the Lord in the air, and so we will always be with the Lord' (1 Thessalonians 4:16–17, CSB).

This will be the full restoration of our humanity and the final defeat of death.

> **1 Corinthians 15:52–55 (CSB):**
>
> **... in a moment, in the twinkling of an eye, at the last trumpet. For the trumpet will sound, and the dead will be raised incorruptible, and we will be changed. For this corruptible body must be clothed with incorruptibility, and this mortal body must be clothed with immortality. When this corruptible body is clothed with incorruptibility, and this mortal body is clothed with immortality, then the saying that is written will take place:**
>
> **Death has been swallowed up in victory.**
> **Where, death, is your victory?**
> **Where, death, is your sting?**

The proof that Jesus is coming again is that He already came in fulfilment of many prophecies past. His first coming was not an accident of history but a fulfilment of ancient promises and prophecies. If He came according to prophecy, then He will surely come again because God's Word is infallible and cannot be broken **(Matthew 5:18).**

The proof of somewhere better than Eden is the fact

that Eden existed. The past allows us to hope for a better future. Think for a moment and imagine Eden ...

2 Peter 3, from **verse 3** and following **(CSB)**, explains it all so well! I would like to break this passage apart, but there is really no need. Please read attentively:

> **Above all, be aware of this: Scoffers will come in the last days scoffing and following their own evil desires, saying, "Where is his 'coming' that he promised? Ever since our ancestors fell asleep, all things continue as they have been since the beginning of creation." They deliberately overlook this: By the word of God the heavens came into being long ago and the earth was brought about from water and through water. Through these the world of that time perished when it was flooded. By the same word, the present heavens and earth are stored up for fire, being kept for the day of judgment and destruction of the ungodly.**
>
> **Dear friends, don't overlook this one fact: With the Lord one day is like a thousand years, and a thousand years like one day. The Lord does not delay his promise, as some understand delay, but is patient with you, not wanting any to perish but all to come to repentance.**
>
> **But the day of the Lord will come like a thief; on that day the heavens will pass away with a loud noise, the elements will burn and be dissolved, and the earth and the works on it will be disclosed. Since all these things are to be dissolved in this way, it is clear what**

> **sort of people you should be in holy conduct and godliness as you wait for the day of God and hasten its coming. Because of that day, the heavens will be dissolved with fire and the elements will melt with heat. But based on his promise, we wait for new heavens and a new earth, where righteousness dwells.**

A summary is this: there will be people who scoff and say that Jesus has been coming 'soon' for over two thousand years and is still not here. However, what they fail to consider is that God does not perceive time as we do, being outside time. He created time, so how could He possibly be bound by it? Rather, He is less concerned with the passing of time than with the repentance of sinners within time.

Indeed, the day is coming when the earth will be consumed by fire, making way for a new Heaven and earth. In light of this, **2 Peter 3** continues in **verses 14–15:**

> **Therefore, dear friends, while you wait for these things, make every effort to be found without spot or blemish in his sight, at peace. Also, regard the patience of our Lord as salvation ...**

While we wait, we must *hasten* the coming of the Lord **(2 Peter 3:12)** by ceaselessly carrying out the ministry of reconciliation God has entrusted to us—proclaiming the Gospel so that sinners may repent **(2 Corinthians 5:19–20)**. This is God's primary concern; it is the reason for His patience, so it must also be our priority while we await the return of Christ.

For many Christians, the coming of Christ does not feel like a realistic expectation. Once, I was having a conversation with a friend about this, and I jokingly said, *'Jesus should wait o!'* thinking of my desire to have a family, among other plans. Her response to my comment made the scales fall from my eyes.

She explained it with an analogy: imagine you're at a wedding where the bridegroom is delayed. Yet the bride seems completely at ease with the wait. In fact, each time she hears that the traffic holding him up has eased, she panics even more. You might think she isn't serious and could walk away from the wedding—even if there was smoky jollof rice.

WELL, are we not the bride of Christ?

> **Revelation 19:7 (CSB)** declares:
> **Let us be glad, rejoice, and give him glory,**
> **because the marriage of the Lamb has come,**
> **and his bride has prepared herself.**

Are we prepared? Are you ready? Or would you prefer to get married, have children and accomplish a few other things before He comes? Are these pursuits more important to you than the ultimate remedy for pain—the hope and restoration His second coming will bring?

Maybe your resistance comes from the negative connotations attached to the word *rapture*. I once had the same fear and used to think of the rapture as being caught off guard, even when I wasn't doing anything wrong. But then, I discovered the meaning of the word rapture: to be filled with intense feelings of pleasure or joy, like the thrill of being reunited with a lover, or when an outfit you imagined turns out perfect in real life—but magnified beyond imagination. This is what we will feel when Jesus returns. We will be completely *enraptured* by the beauty of our Bridegroom, and of course!

The same great joy that heralded the Lord's incarnation will be ours when He returns!

Luke 2:10–14 (NIV):

10 But the angel said to them, "Do not be afraid. I bring you good news that will cause *great joy* for all the people.

11 Today in the town of David a Savior has been born to you; he is the Messiah, the Lord.

12 This will be a sign to you: You will find a baby wrapped in cloths and lying in a manger."

13 Suddenly a great company of the heavenly host appeared with the angel, praising God and saying,

14 *"Glory to God in the highest heaven, and on earth peace to those on whom his favor rests."*

Also, keep this in mind: **'When the Son of Man returns, it will be like it was in Noah's day. In those days before the flood, the people were enjoying banquets and parties and weddings right up to the time Noah entered his boat. People didn't realize what was going to happen until the flood came and swept them all**

away. That is the way it will be when the Son of Man comes' (Matthew 24:37–39, NLT).

The return of Christ is a two-faced event: a day of joy for believers, and for unbelievers, a day of terror. This Day of the Lord will be a day of darkness, not light, for those without Christ standing as their mediator on that day of judgement. It will be a day of anguish, sorrow, darkness and gloom—as if a man escaped from a lion, only to meet a bear **(Amos 5:18; Zephaniah 1:14–18).**

What choice do we have but to be prepared, especially in these last days? If we put God's kingdom first, as we are commanded to in **Matthew 6:33**, everything else must take second place to the priorities of His kingdom.

Nature waits for things to be right again, for the Gospel was preached not just to humanity but to all creation **(Colossians 1:23).**

Romans 8:19–20 (KJV):
19 For the earnest expectation of the creation eagerly waits for the revealing of the sons of God.
20 For the creation was subjected to futility, not willingly, but because of Him who subjected it in hope;

Somewhere better than Eden begins here on earth. A life of communion, reverence, obedience and unbroken fellowship starts in our hearts the moment we accept Christ. It is redemption, not innocence, for our free will once robbed us of the innocence we were given. Now, we have the opportunity to choose rightly—to choose God and life again.

What a beautiful wonder the coming of Jesus will be. **1 Corinthians 13:10, 12 (KJV)** describes it as PERFECT. Yes, perfection is coming!

> **'But when that which is PERFECT is come, then that which is in part shall be done away. For now we see through a glass, darkly; but then FACE to FACE: now I know in part; but then shall I know even as also I am known.'**

We will see God, not face to face as it was described in Moses' time, which referred to the openness and freedom of fellowship Moses enjoyed with God rather than a literal display of God's countenance **(Exodus 33:11; Numbers 12:8)**. We know this because **1 John 4:12** states that no one has ever seen God. Yet we will see Him face to face, in a time when our physical, mortal bodies have been transformed, and we are given the capacity for immortality to commune with God as He is through Jesus, the first Man in Heaven **(John 3:13)**. For Christ has already shown His disciples a glimpse of this redeemed body **(John 21)**, and we will follow in due time, to eternally remain in the presence of God.

We will not see Him as in a mirror anymore, but face to face. '**... we know that, when he shall appear, we shall be like him; for we shall see him as he is' (1 John 3:2, KJV)**. We will see Him clearly! We will fellowship with Him closely and intimately, with no space between us.

What a joy! We, His children, will finally be with our Father. I cannot wait!

If this is the hope of the Christian, you and me, we must not relent in spreading the Good News to all. We must not be ashamed of this Gospel of Christ, for we have been called not only to believe but also to suffer for Jesus. And by His power, we have the boldness to proclaim the goodness of God to all **(Romans 1:16; Philippians 1:29; Acts 4:29–31)**.

Our big dreams must not be defined by material ambition but deep pants for the eternal. We must lift our gaze and be captivated, time and again, by the certain hope that one day, we will be with the Lord!

Unlike the dominion mandate given to Adam, we have something far greater—something that extends beyond this earth. **Hebrews 10:34 (ESV)** says, **'For you had compassion on those in prison, and you joyfully accepted the plundering of your property, since you knew that you yourselves had a better possession and an abiding one.'**

It is the knowledge of what awaits us on the other side that loosens our grip on the material. **Hebrews 11:16 (ESV)** puts it this way: **'But as it is, they desire a better country, that is, a heavenly one. Therefore God is not ashamed to be called their God, for he has prepared for them a city.'**

Indeed, Jesus has gone to prepare a place for us **(John 14:2)** so we can be with Him—this is our inheritance: that we will always be with the Lord, for He is our portion. In the Old Testament, the Levites were set apart to serve as priests in God's temple. This meant they did not receive material possessions, like land, unlike the other tribes of Israel. What did they receive instead? **Joshua 13:33 (CSB)** says, '**But Moses did not give a portion to the tribe of Levi. The Lord, the God of Israel, was their inheritance, just as he had promised them.**' Compare this with **Revelation 1:6**, which declares that Jesus has '**made us ... priests to his God and Father—**'

By our sinless High Priest, we have all been made priests! In this sense, we are all Levites called to serve God by His Spirit. He is our reward, and when the final judgement comes, we will not be ashamed. Instead, we will stand with confidence, for He abides in us **(Matthew 25, 1 John 4:16–17)**.

> **1 Peter 1:3 (CSB):**
> **Therefore, with your minds ready for action, be sober-minded and set your hope *completely* on the GRACE to be brought to you at the revelation of Jesus Christ.**

If we think we have received grace now, we haven't seen anything yet. Greater grace awaits us at the revelation of our King!

May the Holy Spirit help us prepare for the coming of our Lord and open our eyes to the wonder and beauty of the rapture, in Jesus' Name, amen.

Resurrected Bodies

I find it crucial to shed some light on the fate of our bodies when Jesus returns. The Bible is clear on this, to an extent.

Philippians 3:20–21 (ESV):
20 But our citizenship is in heaven, and from it we await a Savior, the Lord Jesus Christ,
21 who will transform our lowly body to be like his glorious body, by the power that enables him even to subject all things to himself.

There is an ongoing sanctification of our inner being in the lives of Christians, a work that will only be completed when Christ returns. However, this completion does not involve our inner selves alone; it extends to our entire being—spirit/soul and body.

The Bible makes it clear that our outer bodies are wasting away, yes. If you think about it pessimistically, each day we live brings us closer to the grave. Yet for the Christian, this is a thing of joy, for it also means we are drawing closer to true, eternal life!

2 Corinthians 4:16–18 (ESV):
16 So we do not lose heart. Though our outer self is wasting away, our inner self is being renewed day by day.
17 For this light momentary affliction is preparing for us an eternal weight of glory beyond all comparison,
18 as we look not to the things that are seen but to the things that are unseen. For the things that are seen are transient, but the things that are unseen are eternal.

This is our hope! 1 Corinthians 15 clarifies that our

bodies are like seeds: what is planted is not as glorious as what will be reaped. The first Adam, formed from dust, bequeathed to us a natural body, subject to decay and death. But the second Adam, who came from Heaven, will give to us, in due time, an immortal and imperishable body, glorious just like His own.

Hold this close to your heart as your feet tread through life on earth.

2 Timothy 2:11–12 (ESV):
If we have died with him, we will also live
with him;
If we endure, we will also reign with him.

Hallelujah!

19

PERSONAL REFLECTIONS

The cross is the sweetest weight ever to fall upon my shoulders.

—Maranatha

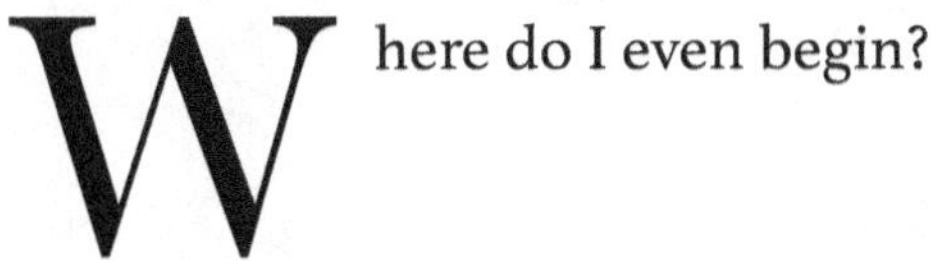

Where do I even begin?

THREE VERSES in the Bible particularly soothe my heart, especially in light of this troublesome world.

The first is **Deuteronomy 23:5**. It says, **'But the Lord your God would not listen to Balaam; instead the Lord your God turned the curse into a blessing for you, because the Lord your God loved you' (ESV).**

The second is **Hebrews 6:13**. It says, **'For when God made a promise to Abraham, since he had no one**

greater by whom to swear, he swore by himself, saying, "Surely I will bless you and multiply you."' (ESV).

The third is **Ephesians 2:3–5**. It says, '**among whom we all once lived in the passions of our flesh, carrying out the desires of the body and the mind, and were by nature children of wrath, like the rest of mankind. But God, being rich in mercy, because of the great love with which he loved us, even when we were dead in our trespasses, made us alive together with Christ—by grace you have been saved—' (ESV).**

In the first verse, God turned Balaam's curses into blessings because of His steadfast love for the children of Israel. In the second, He swore by Himself to Abraham, for there was no one greater by whom to swear. The third emphasised God's immense mercy and love for us, demonstrated through the redeeming work of Christ in our salvation. He did this while we were still dead in our sins, utterly helpless and without hope.

A SONG WELLS up within me:

Oh that men would praise the Lord
Oh that men would praise the Lord
For His goodness and for His wonderful works
To the children of men
To the children of men
He has broken the gates of brass
And cut the bars of iron asunder!

. . .

THESE VERSES, even the song, make my heart ache with the weight of my unworthiness in comparison to God's unshakable and unconditional love for me—for all of humanity.

It makes me ask, for the umpteenth time, WHY? Why does God love us so? The answer is simple yet unfathomable: He cannot help but love us, for He is love. One of my favourite songs about God's redemption of us, *The Blood & The Barley* by Dalton and Anna Thomas, has a line that always fills me with awe:

'You [God] love to forgive
You delight in mercy.'

God's love is His forgiveness. It is because He loves me that He forgave my sins and restored my access to Him through His Son. Without His forgiveness, His love could not be fully expressed. And He is not forgiving because He *has* to—if there is anyone who truly does not *have to* do anything, it is God, for He is God. On the contrary, God loves to forgive! He delights in showing mercy.

There I am, often wrestling with unforgiveness, ruminating over offences even when my offender has apologised. Then there is God, who is always seeking whom to forgive, always looking to extend mercy. How wondrous! I need to be like my God.

In the stories of the lost son, sheep and coin **(Luke 15)**, the first mover was God. I think of the Ninevites, how God called Jonah, not once, but twice, to go and preach to them so that they might repent and receive His forgiveness. I think of Ahab, that notorious king of whom it was said, **'There was none who sold himself to do what was evil in the sight of the Lord like Ahab, whom Jezebel his wife incited.'** Yet, notice God's delight at Ahab's repentance; He was a beaming Father! He said, **'Have you seen how Ahab has humbled himself before me? Because he has humbled himself before me, I will not bring the disaster in his days; but in his son's days I will bring the disaster upon his house' (1 Kings 21:25, 29, ESV).**

Is it not the same in all our stories? Which of us came to God by ourselves? Our inflated egos make us think we have some goodness in us. But how can we do any good when we sin simply by being? Jonathan Edwards puts it strikingly, *'You contribute nothing to your salvation except the sin that made it necessary.'* God had to rescue us; there was no other way out of the depravity of our minds. It's incredible. God is cool, so cool.

When I was a vile offender, I couldn't contemplate Heaven. I didn't want it, because my sinful nature did not know how to long for something truly good. Now, I think of Heaven and I long for it. I long for lasting peace and a life devoid of anger, pain, distractions, the constant search for direction, and all of earth's turmoil. The earth, despite the Fall, still holds much good; God has lavished many common graces upon all creation. And yet, my soul finds no lasting satisfaction in it, for it was never meant to.

Something is aching within me. Indeed, He has put eternity in my heart **(Ecclesiastes 3:11).** And no wonder, can anything in this mortal world satisfy an immortal soul?

'You have made us for yourself, O Lord, and our heart is restless until it rests in you.'[1]

WHAT I LONG FOR is not a place, it's a Person. And it is only because of Him that I am considered worthy to be in His presence.

It is God that I long for. The Lord Almighty. The Holy One. I often wonder what He is like. I wonder what it will be like to gaze upon the face of Love itself. I wonder if my being will be able to contain—or adequately express—the overwhelming joy of existing in the same space with the One who looked at my sorry, filthy, sinful self and declared, *'I will die for you.'*

Even as I write this, my eyes water. I lived over twenty years of my life without God. *What patience is this?* It is the remembrance of His faithfulness that softens my heart towards others and shapes the rhythm of my entire life. At least, I try to let it.

It is not easy.

Being like God is no small quest—what a lofty standard!

It is a call to activity, rather than passivity.

It is a call to love actively, seeking every opportunity to do good to others, even as I pursue the glorification of God.

It is a call to wait actively, praising God for what I have and expressing joyful expectation for what I desire, rather than anxiously hovering, pretending not to care, while peeping to see if my prayers will be answered.

---

1. Attributed to St Augustine.

It is a call to die actively, for God Himself did not hold back on that cross. For there He declared, by His sacrifice, *'I love you, and with all of myself.'* So, I cannot be like God by clinging to myself. In fact, I must despise my autonomy and yield to His sovereignty over every inch of my life.

Who can be like God if they have not first been broken apart by Him? Who can reflect His glory if He does not lend us a portion of Himself to animate us, renew our desires and yet command within us what He desires?

What an unattainable standard! Only the Standard Himself can help me. For my calling is not an aversion to pleasure or pain, comfort or joy, riches or poverty, but to turn from whatever it is that does not inspire godly, edifying thoughts—thoughts that are true, pure, honourable, lovely and worthy of praise—or that fail to bring a smile to my King's face, when He looks upon me.

My calling is to give myself completely to the One who gave Himself completely for me. My call is to holiness, as He is holy. And holiness is not just something we say, it is something we do; it is what we are called to be.

It is easy to throw the word 'service' around. It is easy to exhort and tell people to lay down their lives as Jesus did. But it is not easy to put the needs of others before my own, to deprioritise being right in favour of being loving and gracious. It is not easy to die.

It helps, then, that the Christian is not called to a life of ease. Jesus often emphasised the cost of following Him—it will cost our lives.

If I follow Him, here is my litmus test:

If I compare my service to His, do I find similarities?

Am I gentle like He is?

Do I serve with joy or murmuring?

Do I serve when it is due or when it is convenient?

Do I actively seek opportunities to serve, or pass them by when they don't fit my schedule?

Our lives can often become the barrier that separates us from God. I think of my daily living—the responsibility of family, work, and community. It takes God to remember not to strive in my own strength. It takes God's help to look up, over and again, and remain longing for Heaven. It takes God to remember that my family, work, friendships, and every other thing I find in my hands, are not determinants of my future, but tools to draw me closer to my God that I might look like Him.

Kehinde once pointed out to me that God's provision is never just for the sake of provision. Beneath the surface [if we will look], every gift, every answer, every miracle is designed to lead us to a deeper revelation of God. Essentially, He gives so that we may be conformed more into His image, through a greater understanding of His character.

This is especially true for suffering. Especially true.

I remember a time when I had an urgent need that I'd been praying about. This wasn't a want, it was a severe need on which other aspects of my life were hinged. As a practical person, my petitions were marked by my proffering of the options I felt God could choose from to answer me, and this was usually the norm. Imagine my surprise when none of my ideas came to pass.

One Sunday, as I sat in the pew, the sermon pierced through my heart, and I realised that, for the first time in a long time, I was in a situation where I had no option but

God. I had come to the end of my imagination, and it was the hardest thing. My vision blurred as I saw how I'd made God small in my eyes. I despaired because I couldn't figure out how things were going to work out.

The same God who does exceedingly, abundantly above all I can ask?

Who was I to imagine His ways?

The good thing is that it was a great place to be. A place of total dependency on God is the best, most secure place for a Christian to dwell. But it was also a scary place to be when one examines the material repercussions.

In my case, I feared what would happen if I didn't get what I needed at the time it was due. I feared it would be summarised by others as a lack of wisdom, for I was also at fault for a deficiency in preparation.

I failed to realise that true folly was not knowing what God wanted. True folly was not pausing to ask, *'But what does God think?'* Beyond asking God to lead us, I think it is also very good to ponder what He thinks. Like a soldier at war, it is easy to take instructions and move. It is harder to act in more nuanced situations based on what you believe your Commanding Officer would prescribe—yet the latter would demonstrate a higher degree of understanding of the C.O.'s ways. This is what I want to have with God, to know His ways and think like Him.

And indeed, isn't the life I live a matter of survival? Hearing from God is a matter of survival. To be cut off from my source is death.

But guess what? God knows exactly how much suffering or blessing each of His children needs to conform to His image, our true end, for God is our highest good. And even when my current suffering persists, I must remember that God is my ultimate deliverance from evil. And this hope is sure. In the Holy Ghost, I have an assurance.

Think of Abraham, poised to sacrifice his son, when God provided a ram in Isaac's place. Abraham returned not only with his son alive, but with a revelation of God as *Jehovah Jireh*, the Provider. Consider Hagar, fleeing into the desert from Sarai's harsh treatment. Surely she needed food, water and shelter—but what did God give her beyond these necessities? A revelation of Himself as *El-Roi*, the God who sees. Think also of Job, who suffered loss at the hands of the accuser [Satan] and wrestled with self-righteousness. When the Lord finally answered him, Job responded in awe: **'My ears had heard of you but now my eyes have seen you. Therefore I despise myself and repent in dust and ashes' (Job 42:5–6, NIV).**

I believe this tells me something that I pray my Lord continually reminds me of: my faith is my most valuable treasure. It is the knowledge of God's character that keeps me grounded. Yes, today I might receive food, and tomorrow a laptop, as the Lord faithfully supplies my needs, but I must learn to see beyond these fleeting things, to pursue a deeper comprehension of God and of all things godly.

And if, perhaps, this comprehension comes through God withholding some of the things that I ask for, then so be it. Every grief, every loss, every moment of waiting is an instrument in the refinement of my faith, with the end of glorifying Jesus.

I pray that the Lord helps me to desire what is truly good for me. I pray He helps me live slowly enough to remember Him. I trust Him to preserve, strengthen and purify my faith, so that when He comes, I will see Him—and be found ready, longing, and filled with joy.

I think of God as a pleased Father who delights in me, His child. When I was younger, I always wished I had richer parents. I dreamed of a day when I would be woken up and summoned to the sitting room, where men in black flanked a figure draped in richly embroidered *agbada*[2], who had come to claim me as his real daughter. I'd watched so many movies with similar plots, and I thought it would be fancy. I longed to have a will read aloud upon my parents' passing, allotting properties or a lump sum of money to me as a testament to their love and care for me. Well, while I certainly am the biological daughter of my parents, I have a Father far greater—a Father who desires that I inherit all that He has for me! His inheritance is not measured in gold or silver, but in eternal riches, unending joy, and the fullness of His presence.

How do I get there? How does anyone get there?

If the Ten Commandments are a transcript of God's character, then the Gospel—living, breathing Jesus—is the true transcript of humanity, teaching me to be human according to God's standards. I find myself, the real me,

2. Agbada is a traditional, flowing, wide-sleeved attire, worn by men, particularly among the Yoruba people in West Africa.

when I look at Jesus. If I can correctly align with the Word, then I am aligned with God.

The world I live in is filled with shifting ideas of what is right and wrong. It helps to remember that my life is not my own, and I no longer exist to please men; otherwise, I would not be a follower of Christ **(Galatians 1:10)**.

I have counted the cost of following Jesus, and it is indeed very high. From the very beginning, it cost me my life and the person I thought I loved most. My heart felt torn within me, my flesh ached, and all I wanted was to appease it to escape the pain. Somehow, I said no. He helped me say no to my flesh and yes to Him. In that moment, I won, but I also died, and it felt like the pain would end me. But it did not. I cried and cried, and the next day, I compared what I had lost with what I had gained in Christ. Then I wept again, but this time, with tears of joy.

That was in 2021. It is 2025 now as I write this, and carrying this cross given to me by Jesus is tremendously light compared to the burden the enemy once laid upon my back. I have lost friends and more along the way, yet every loss has drawn me to a greater portion of my Lord. And truly, what is the loss of earthly things in life when I already lost my own life at the beginning? It is incomparable.

God has tested me to know my fitness for His use. I have failed many times, but I have also passed many times —I think. I have been diligent in my zeal, fervent in the Spirit and steadfast in serving my Lord. I have done this not because I am anything special, but solely because of His mercies.

In that dark pit from which my Lord rescued me, there were many others still trapped. Sometimes, I see someone I once knew from the pit now walking on the side of light where I stand, and my heart melts again at His goodness. *'Oh, Jesus rescued you, too!'* I cry out in glee. But there are still so many more left in the pit. I have tried, in my strength, to stretch a hand to pull a man out, but he almost dragged me back in. I relented and went to ask my Lord for strength. He asked me to be still and behold His salvation.

My Lord is exceedingly kind to me. He is the sweetest Person that I know. Every day, when I pray, I come to know Him more deeply, and our love grows ever sweeter. I used to struggle to spend time with God in the mornings as a habit, but when I saw how my decision-making and perspective improved throughout the day simply because I spoke first to my Lord upon waking, I could not stop.

One morning, as I studied my Bible, my heart lingered on a Scripture: '**Love is patient ...**' from **1 Corinthians 13.** I had read it countless times, yet that morning it would not let me go. As it turned out, I needed a greater measure of patience for that day, and my Lord met me right where I was, giving it through His Word the moment my eyes welcomed the day. I wept sweetly as I realised His tender provision. What a sweet, sweet Lover I have in my Jesus.

Sometimes, my Lord nudges me to reach out to someone I haven't spoken to in a while. In the shower, He reminds me to share the Gospel with my Uber driver on the way out and not to forget the evangelism tracts in my bag. Every day, He grants me spiritual insight so that yesterday's blessings do not become today's curse.

So, every morning, the unforgiveness and bitterness fall away, and the need to be right gives way to love. I recite **1 Corinthians 13:4–7**, notice all the ways I've fallen short, and repent.

I have killed my flesh many times, and each death is worse than the previous. In 2018, in a church at school, a minister called me, sat me down, and asked me to delete all the worldly songs on my phone. I laughed and walked away. Years later, with tears blurring my eyes, I swiped through my Apple Music for hours until every song that made my flesh rejoice was gone.

The Holy Spirit indeed leads us to all truth. He led me to so many truths about my life that I had long buried. Truly, a person cannot see himself clearly unless he has seen God.

The kingdom of Heaven is like a treasure hidden in a field, which a man discovers. Overjoyed, he goes and sells everything he has to acquire the field in which the treasure lies **(Matthew 13:44)**. This is a treasure that I have found, and I am proud to have.

Sometimes, the world tries to make me feel guilty for possessing this treasure. But it is a treasure! How could I feel bad for having something so good? I have made the decision to show off my Abba, not only in the good stuff but also in the hard stuff. As Job declared, I will not accept only good from God, but also adversity **(Job 2:10)**. I trust His love in what He allows, for He knows best.

I know that if I follow God, He will lead me to all the places I need to be. I call Him The Arranger for a reason. My Abba pays attention to the tiniest of details when it comes to me.

I enjoy praying to God, not just to see as He does, but to bring before Him all my needs and wants. Isn't a request sweeter when there is a knowing that the answer is going to be good **(Romans 8:32)**? As I grow to resemble my Father, I also depend on Him for all things.

I think it is false spirituality for one to think that we should bring before God only prayers for spiritual growth, as if petitioning for the material matters of our lives is somehow ungodly or less *spiritual*. No. I will ask for all things from my Father, who will not withhold any good thing from me. He never wavers in His care; He is faithful, steadfast, and wholly responsible for me.

If God wanted me to only be spiritual, in that sense, He would have made me a spiritual being or an angel. Instead, He made me human; wholly human!

He gives richly to me for my enjoyment—from the mundane to the extraordinary. This is a gift as much as it is a responsibility; I must act in a manner pleasing to God, steward all He has given me, and really, *really* enjoy these gifts with love and joy in my heart to His glory. Life is not to be endured but enjoyed; it is to be lived in communion with God, appreciating the beauty He has woven into every moment.

A major aspect of following Jesus is self-denial. There is no '*living a life that is mine*' because my life ceased to be mine when I accepted Christ. I cannot be *me*—the self-centred, prideful, rebellious me—because my true identity now is Him.

The calling is to look like Him **(Ephesians 5:1)**. This is what God wants; it is His will. To live otherwise is, the Bible judges, folly—failing to discern what the Lord wants from me **(Ephesians 5:17)**. The beauty, and I dare say mystery, in Christ is that I can be fully in Him, look like Him, and still stand out in a world of over seven billion people. Truly, seeing Him allows me to see myself—the real me, not the mask I once wore, not the desires that once enslaved me.

In Him, I find my true form, my true purpose, my true life.

I know that every action taken to please God is rewarded **(Galatians 6:8)**. He does not overlook the small, sincere efforts of His children. When babies try to walk, and they stumble, do we not applaud them? How much more does my Abba and King, also, delight in—and reward—my little steps towards Him. Our imperfect steps are treasured and multiplied by the One who holds all things in His hand.

But babies must grow. If a child refuses to grow, it defies the life inside of it. Life is not only a state of being but a progression of being. If a child of five decides to remain crawling instead of walking, it stops being cute and becomes a concern. There is no applause but serious prayers.

Yet, I must learn to discern my part from God's. He works according to His timing, method and purpose. If only I could learn to actively wait for Him, constantly praying and seeking Him, despite my many troubles. Only then will my eyes be opened to perceive the power and might of God, because whether I believe it or not, God is mighty. The question is, will I recognise His might when it is displayed in my life? I pray I do.

I desire to spend my days well. I'm learning to number

them **(Psalm 90:12)**. I want no phase of my life to be blurry, in a hurry, or to be squandered waiting for a *better* tomorrow because that better tomorrow is already today. My future is here, now.

MY PRAYER IS THIS:

> *Help me live it out for You, Lord, in worship of You, to the glory of Your Name. Even as I move from assignment to assignment in fulfilment of Your purpose for me, I contain joy, and I spread You still. I am not stagnant. I am full of life and goodness from You. I live life without regrets but redeem the time* ***(Ephesians 5:16)*** *because the days are evil, and I must make the most of every day before I leave here to be with You. Help me do so, in Jesus' Name,*
>
> *amen.*

What can the world offer me that there isn't already an abundance of in His presence? I look forward to standing before God, awe-filled and trembling at His glory, but justified and unafraid of His judgement.

I would rather be beaten with a stick and pelted with stones for the sake of my faith—for that would prove my faith to be a serious thing—than to be mocked with careless, unserious words, for that might make my faith seem a funny, laughable thing. And I find nothing laughable about Christ's love for me.

I see that the best use of my time on this earth is to prepare for my life to come. Viewing life through the lens of eternity moves me to the ministry of reconciliation (1

Timothy 2:4), to bring as many with me as possible. Is the harvest not ready? I pray the Lord of the harvest to send in even more labourers!

My happiness in life is tied not to fleeting pleasures or human approval, but to pleasing God according to His Word, not my preconceived notions. He is my vitality. To see Him more and never cease looking is my deepest desire. To become like Him, a little more each day, is the goal I chase. Looking at God always has the effect of deadening the desires of the world. My heart longs for this daily transformation.

I often reflect on the transience of life. The vanity. The brevity. How easy it is, in a world so vast, to feel so small. I am blessed to have God, who gives purpose to my days, to make my life count for something.

I get tired, too. I'm thinking of how God holds the length of my days in His hands. I think to ask God, '*Am I living a good life by Your standards?*' and I can imagine His response already, 'YOU GET TO CHOOSE NOW.' I want to finish the work He has sent me here to do. I must redeem the time, for the days are evil.

Sometimes, I look back at those times I was not serious in my walk with God, when I missed all the times He moved. I was a spectator then, but what an honour it is now to be a participant!

> *All these years I spent not knowing You, yet You waited. Some will never accept You until their deathbeds, and still, You say yes. Something spectacular must be on the other side of this life, then. Something beyond my mind's comprehension must be on the other side of this world, and You do not want any of*

Your children to miss it. How I long to see what is on the other side. I cannot wait.

I have found myself pondering Heaven more than before, reflecting on life here on earth. If God were to call me home today, I would be ready. It would hurt, yes, but living or dying is still Jesus, so it is no loss. I am learning to loosen my grip on the things of this world, travelling light, unattached. Not attached.

The more material possessions I acquire, the more boxes I tick off my checklist, the more I have to consciously remind myself to keep my eyes on Heaven and not focus on accumulating more stuff. Comfort is good, but it is not primary.

I am living consciously of every moment. Present. Mindful.

Life is already short, so why rush through it?

There's nothing to do but be here.

So, I'll be here.

I will *be*.

I will laugh every laugh to its end, till it dies a natural death in my belly. I will smile until it reaches my eyes.

No interruptions, just living; matching forward thinking with mindful living. The future is only the accumulated fullness of every present I have ever lived, whether good or bad.

I really enjoy praying and spending time with Jesus. There is something truly amazing about *staying*. Even when it feels like I have nothing to say, just singing, meditating, or reflecting on Him fills me. It is the staying that moulds me to His will, really. It is how I learn to listen in the quiet—and even in the noise too.

Something about God bringing the animals to Adam so he could name them shattered every pre-salvific notion I had of Him as a tyrant or the big, unconcerned, controlling 'guy up there.' All I see now is a Creator delighted in His creation, overflowing with love, intimacy and fellowship. My goodness!

Matthew 11:29 opens my eyes to a God who is as powerful as He is humble. God does not merely wield power, He is power. Just as He is love and He is goodness. He is the bar. He is the standard. He's the perfect embodiment of every goodness in this world. Every virtue is perfectly expressed in Him.

I marvel at how God could have simply erased our sins without consequence, yet He chose instead to uphold His perfect principle that sin must be punished by death **(Romans 6:23)**. He could have made humanity dumb, stripped of free will, and incapable of questioning Him so that none of us would have ever doubted or sinned. But He did not. He is not afraid of my questions or human logic because He is Truth. His desire is not for blind obedience, but that people come to know Him and the knowledge of the truth. He wants us to see, to choose, and to be saved. Not by coercion, but by love and understanding.

Today, Lord, I thank You for opening my eyes.
It is truly Your way to conceal and mine to search ***(Proverbs 25:2)****.*
Never stop opening my eyes, Lord.

Let me see as You see.
May my heart always perceive the wonders of Your love, the depth of Your justice, and the beauty of Your ways.

There's this human tendency to want everything figured out, to have a mental manual so that I can always go through the motions without pause, rather than refer to authority whenever I feel low or need guidance. Yet, Jesus calls me to something deeper: to be in sync with Him, moment by moment. He desires that I return to Him constantly, rather than leaning on my own wisdom. My life is not meant to follow my plans alone; it is meant to flow in constant communion with Him.

He wants me to know that I know *nothing*—that my knowledge, my plans, and my understanding are small and fleeting—and should know nothing but Him, who is everything. In surrender, in worship, in paying attention, in prayer and Bible study, in devotion, in gifts, in listening, in serving, in ministry, in works, in purpose—it is all Him.

It is YOU I seek after. YOU.

Even what I think I know requires daily renewal from His Spirit, so the flesh does not taint it. I must depend on God because my life depends on Him. Jesus does not want performance. He wants me in the now, vulnerable, honest, and fully present, not wearing the mask from yesterday because that devotion felt much more *intense* or *emotional.*

If only I come to God, He'll take care of the rest. It is the only condition, yet people do not see. '**Harden the hearts of these people. Plug their ears and shut their**

eyes. That way, they will not see with their eyes, nor hear with their ears, nor understand with their hearts and turn to me for healing' (Isaiah 6:10, NLT).

How tragic that so many remain blind to the simplicity of His call.

Perhaps, the greatest revelation of purpose is realising that I have none. This is why His call is so simple. It is God's purpose that I carry. The Christian call—to belong to one another and live out God's love—does not come naturally, for sin has marred our hearts and clouded our instincts. Yet, through grace, it is possible. I, we, are called to be an extension of God's kindness, living vessels that reflect His mercy and lead others to repentance and restoration.

God does not need me; God wants me. That should give perspective that, ideally, reclaiming us would not have been a do-or-die affair. Yet for Him, who is love, it became so.

> **'But the jar he was making did not turn out as he had hoped, so he crushed it into a lump of clay again and started over' (Jeremiah 18:4–6, NLT).**

This is His *moulding* of me. God is not trying to hurt me; He is trying to *kill* me. Again and again, He crushes and remakes me, refining me into something beautiful. May He help me bend willingly to His hands.

If I could tell anyone anything, beyond good advice or motivational talk, it would be this: *Allow God to do what He brought you here for*. This is the core of our existence, from footballers to musicians.

Our purpose is to glorify God through our lives. It is to turn from ourselves and the self-centred impulses that constantly tug at our thoughts and actions, and to yield our entire beings to Him. In other words, it is not about us; it is about Him.

Just as the moon reflects the brilliance of the sun, our lives are to reflect the radiance of who God is and all that He has done.

While Jesus is representing me in heaven, may I reflect him on earth.[3]

We do this by pointing others away from ourselves and towards Him; by sharing what He has done, most importantly through the Gospel; by trusting Him through our trials; by walking in obedience to His will; and by abiding in a soul-satisfying relationship with Him. And the opportunities for this are endless, for He is infinitely glorious in both who He is and what He does.

Could there be any greater purpose for existing than the one God has given us?

And God is looking *too*. He is El-roi. What does He see when He looks at me?

I hope I remain conscious of His constant presence, listening for His voice, and always obeying His bidding. I hope I remember that His gaze rests on me while I live, walk, and *be*. I hope my daily life presents numerous occasions for Him to smile on me, again and again.

. . .

3. God Enjoyed: *The Valley of Vision*, Arthur Bennett.

To my reader, I hope you do the same. I hope you remember that you always have the choice to look at God and let your gaze remain. Even when the enemy whispers wicked thoughts in your head, as he did to Eve to eat the fruit, or to Job in his suffering to curse God and die ... you still have the choice to say no. The enemy's power lies merely in his suggestions. He could not have forced the fruit into Eve's mouth.

Always remember: you are not missing out on anything in the world by being in God. Lean on your Father. He means everything He says, and He will perform it. Trust Him. The more you look at God, the more you look like Him. The more you look like Him, the more you look like you; who you were made to be ... who you were created to be.

Once, at a community hangout, we discussed God's grace, and I realised it was something I'd never truly pondered. I checked the dictionary, and two words stood out: kindness and indulgence. This is what I mean when I say 'by the grace of God.' His kindness is evident in His love, empowerment, mercy, and discipline to ensure that I do not stray from the straight path. His indulgence is the doting care and admiration a child can only get from a Father who adores her and is satisfied with her for just being herself; no performances or extras required.

I am in the position of a beloved child. I will remain.

Will you?

A NOTE TO YOU, MY SIBLING

God is a circle whose centre is everywhere, and whose circumference is nowhere—an inexhaustible portion is He.[1]

If you missed it, the Message is Christ. If, for some reason, you do not know Him as intimately as you know you should, I give you this Message of reconciliation. Jesus wants you, and now—tomorrow is too far!

Romans 10:9:
if thou shalt confess with thy mouth the Lord Jesus, and shalt believe in thine heart that God hath raised him from the dead, thou shalt be saved.

1. *Thomas Brooke: An Ark for all of God's Noah.*

Feel free to email me at mara@visitmaranatha.com if you would like some help on your new journey.

More than anything, I hope you come into an understanding and acceptance of God as your Father, far more intimately than you ever have. I would love to hear from you, too: reviews, questions, contributions, testimonies—everything!

If this book affected your life in any way, please consider leaving me a quick review. Just a few words will do. Your review might encourage another reader to take a chance on this work. To leave a review, please visit Goodreads: https://www.goodreads.com/book/show/250460280-look-at-god-look-like-god

You can also sign up for my mailing list here: https://maranathammxxi.kit.com/maranathasletters

Access a library of my other books by scanning the QR code below:

Visitmaranatha.com

Visitmaranatha.com

See you shortly,
Your sister, Maranatha.

OTHER WORKS

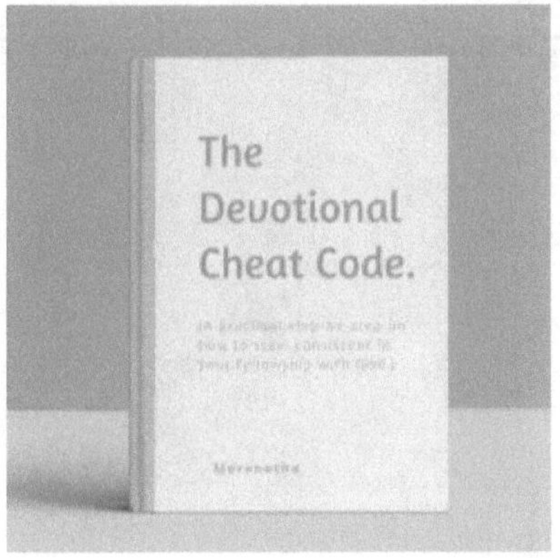

The Devotional Cheat Code: A practical step-by-step on how to stay consistent in your devotion to God: A book with practical and easily applicable 'cheats' for anyone struggling with consistency in their devotion to and fellowship with God.

ALL YOU HAVE to be is Light: This book gets rid of common Christian stereotypes. It connects personal/character development to the spread of the Gospel, highlighting the importance of evangelism for all Christians.

STAYING SOFT: Poems to restore your heart to softness in Christ: a Christian poetry anthology—100 poems (11 written in Igbo) and illustrations—designed to uplift your heart, convert your soul and draw your spirit closer to God through relatable stories (and traumas) that we all share and carry.

. . .

You can get these books at Visitmaranatha.com.

ABOUT THE AUTHOR

Ogonna 'Maranatha' Nnaemeka is a servant who is dedicated to her Father's Work—*'Who wants all people to be saved and come to the knowledge of the truth.'*

She does this by writing soul-piercing and intimate pieces that help people slow down enough to think about God, and perhaps look at Him. She also runs a blog on Visitmaranatha.com, where she shares personal experiences in her walk of faith, as well as resources to help Christians grow in their faith.

Look at God Look like God is her fourth published book.

Website: Visitmaranatha.com
Newsletter: maranathammxxi.kit.com/maranathasletters
Instagram: Instagram.com/maranatha._/
Mail: Mara@visitmaranatha.com
Goodreads: Goodreads.com/au-
thor/show/54840348.Maranatha

ABOUT THE BOOK

Look at God Look like God is a book about maturing in resemblance to Christ—serving the true God by beholding Him and Him alone. It is what He made us and has saved us for: to look like Him by conforming to the image of Christ. The question is: How do we grow in this resemblance in our daily, mundane living?

Broken into three parts: Creation, Distortion and Conformity, it tells the simple but powerful story of God's original plan for humanity (Creation), the fall of humanity and our losing sight of God (Distortion), and the incarnation of God as Jesus Christ, through whom every believer regains access to God, and is empowered to live above sin by gazing steadily at Him to regain our true identity (conformity).

The book will guide readers to understand what it means to be created in the image of God—revealing how we bear the likeness of our Abba Father more deeply than we could ever dare to imagine. Embracing this reality unlocks a richer experience of God's Fatherhood, cultivates daily intimacy with Him, and keeps our gazes tilted heavenward with respect to the Second Coming of Jesus, our ultimate desire.

For the fatherless and the ones who have yet to experience the fullness of true intimacy in paternity. This book illuminates the path to seeing God clearly, reflecting Him authentically, and living in the freedom of His gift of salvation.

www.ingramcontent.com/pod-product-compliance
Lightning Source LLC
LaVergne TN
LVHW100522110826
845146LV00002B/743

* 9 7 9 8 9 8 7 1 7 4 2 5 8 *